AAT

Technician Level 4

Unit 15

Cash Management and Credit Control

WORKBOOK

1175/A01

British Library Cataloguing-in-Publication Data

A catalogue record for this book is available from the British Library.

Published by Foulks Lynch Ltd
4, The Griffin Centre
Staines Road
Feltham
Middlesex
TW14 0HS

ISBN   0 7483 5117 5

© Foulks Lynch Ltd, 2001

Printed and bound in Great Britain by Ashford Colour Press, Gosport, Hants.

Acknowledgements

We are grateful to the Association of Accounting Technicians, the Association of Chartered Certified Accountants, the Chartered Institute of Management Accountants and the Institute of Chartered Accountants in England and Wales for permission to reproduce past assessment and examination questions. The answers have been prepared by Foulks Lynch Ltd. The copyright to the questions remains with the examining body.

CONTENTS

PREFACE

Page

iv

Questions   *Answers*

SPECIMEN SIMULATION

1   25

CHAPTER ACTIVITIES

PRACTICE ASSESSMENT ACTIVITIES

CLASS ACTIVITIES FOR COLLEGES

PREFACE

This is the 2001 edition of the AAT workbook for Unit 15 – Cash Management and Credit Control. The workbook includes the sample simulation provided by the AAT.

The workbook has been produced to complement our Unit 15 textbook and it contains numerous practice questions and tasks designed to reflect and simulate the work place environment. These are arranged to match the chapters of the textbook, so that you can work through the two books together.

The workbook also contains practice assessment activities to prepare you completely for the assessment procedures which form part of your course.

Fully comprehensive answers to all questions, tasks and assessments are provided, with the exception of those which are designated as being specifically for classroom work.

You will find that completion of all the elements of this workbook will prepare you admirably for the assessments which you must carry out to pass Unit 15.

Class Activities

A feature of this workbook is the section at the end comprising Activities which are specially designed for classroom use. The answers to these are not included in the workbook but are reproduced in the new College Kit which is available to college lecturers who adopt our material.

New College Kits

In addition to the Textbooks and Workbooks, Foulks Lynch offers colleges adopting our material the new 'College Kits'.

The College Kits for units with a Devolved Assessment contain:

- additional Devolved Assessment material in looseleaf form which can be photocopied to provide practice classwork for students (much of this additional Assessment material is taken from the AAT's own Assessments); and

- the looseleaf answers to the class examples from the Workbooks.

These Kits are supplied at no extra cost and may be photocopied under the limited licence which is granted to adopting colleges.

TECHNICIAN STAGE

NVQ/SVQ LEVEL 4 IN ACCOUNTING

REVISED STANDARDS
SPECIMEN SIMULATION

OPERATING A CASH MANAGEMENT AND
CREDIT CONTROL SYSTEM

(UNIT 15)

FOULKSlynch

ASSOCIATION OF ACCOUNTING TECHNICIANS

DATA AND TASKS

INSTRUCTIONS

This simulation is designed to test your ability to operate a cash management and credit control system.

The situation is set out on page 3.

The tasks for you to perform are detailed on pages 4 - 5.

You are allowed **four hours** to complete your work.

A high level of accuracy is required. Check your work carefully before handing it in.

Correcting fluid may be used but it should be used in moderation. Any errors should be crossed out neatly and clearly. The use of pencils for your written answers is not acceptable.

You should read the whole simulation before commencing work so as to gain an overall picture of what is required.

Write your answers in the separate answer booklet provided. Paper for rough work is provided on page 24 of the answer booklet. If you need any additional paper ask the person in charge.

You are reminded that you should not bring any unauthorised material, such as books or notes, into the simulation. If you have any such material in your possession, you should surrender it to the assessor immediately.

Any instances of misconduct will be brought to the attention of the AAT, and disciplinary action may be taken.

THE SITUATION

Your name is Jaymini Patel and you work as an accounts clerk for Blether Telecom. The company is an independent telephone brokerage for fixed telephones. It claims to offer customers savings of up to 30 percent off national and international calls. The system works by re-programming a customer's switchboard, enabling Blether Telecom to switch between the different telecommunications carriers according to which operator is offering the best deal that month.

Personnel involved in the scenario:

Accounts Clerk: Yourself, Jaymini Patel
Cash Manager: Douglas Gulland
Credit Controller: Millie Will
Financial Controller: Firdu Gomal

◇ **FOULKS***lynch*

TASKS TO BE PERFORMED

Control cash receipts and payments

1.   Refer to the budget data sheet on pages 6 to 7 of this simulation. The date is 1 December 1997. You are required to use this information to produce a cash forecast for Blether Telecom for the period to 31 March 1998. The cash forecast should clearly show the opening and closing cash position for each month, as well as the net cash flow for the period. The forecast should be prepared in the answer booklet on page 11. It might help you to complete a table of estimated call volumes before calculating revenues and costs. A table for this is also provided on page 11 of your answer booklet.

2.   Analyse the cash flow forecast prepared in Task 1. Using page 12 in the answer booklet, briefly describe how the forecast cash position should be managed. Also identify THREE legitimate measures that Blether Telecom can take to improve the cash position giving a reason for each.

3.   What other cash flow items have been possibly excluded from this cash flow forecast? Using page 13 in the answer booklet identify FOUR items and, for each one, an appropriate individual in the organisation (not necessarily named in the scenario) who could provide this information.

Manage cash balances

4.   Consider the cash flow forecast produced in task 1. Identify the control action required (if any), and the timing of that action, in respect of this forecast. Write your answer in the form of an e-mail note to Douglas Gulland in your answer booklet on page 14.

5.   It is likely that within eighteen months, Blether Telecom will be forecasting a cash surplus. As a growing organisation, Blether Telecom has already negotiated short-term borrowing facilities but has little experience of investing cash. Douglas Gulland has asked you to prepare a presentation for the benefit of the senior management group. The presentation should include the following:

  •   introduction: why a policy for managing investments is required;
  •   the main criteria to be considered when investing cash;
  •   the main types of cash investments available, and a brief description of each;
  •   the main types of marketable securities suitable for short-term investment;
  •   summary; an outline policy for Blether Telecom.

Your presentation should be prepared in note form, outlining the relevant details for each of the points. You should prepare notes for a presentation to last no more than 10 minutes. Use the blank pages 15 - 16 in the answer booklet for this task.

Grant credit

6.   A new customer, MetalBash plc, wishes to contract with Blether Telecom to provide its telephone services. It wishes to do this on 60 days credit. Blether Telecom's credit policy requires a satisfactory credit analysis based on the potential customer's trading record. An extract from MetalBash's accounts for the four years to 31.03.97 is reproduced on page 8. Using these accounts calculate the following ratios for the three years to 31.03.97:
  •   working capital: total assets;
  •   no credit interval (debtors plus cash and short-term investments: daily operating expenses, excluding depreciation);
  •   retained earnings: total assets;
  •   earnings before interest and taxation: interest charges plus annual repayment of loans.

The ratios should be inserted in the answer booklet on page 17.

7. Write a brief memo to Millie Will to identify:
    - the meaning and purpose of the ratios;
    - the trends in these four ratios for the three years to 31 March 1997;
    - whether Blether Telecom should grant credit and/or trade with MetalBash.

    Your memo should be written on page 18 of the answer booklet.

8. After completing your credit review, and discussing the position with Millie Will, MetalBash have telephoned you to establish as to whether you will be granting them credit. How will you respond? Write your answer in the answer booklet on page 19.

Collection of debts

9. An extract from Blether Telecom's aged analysis of debtors as at 31 October 1997 is shown on page 9. Update the analysis as at 30 November 1997, including the transactions shown on page 10. The analysis to be updated is shown in the answer booklet on page 20.

    Each of the five customers is profiled briefly on page 10. For each of the five debtors, outline an appropriate action to manage the account, using page 21 in the answer booklet.

10. John Chancer, a sole trader, has traded with Blether Telecom for four months but has not paid for any of the calls made. Total debts stand at £861.00. Millie Will has suggested that Blether Telecom have Chancer declared bankrupt, but isn't sure how effective this action might be. You are scheduled to meet Millie later that week. Write notes for her attention, using blank page 23 in the answer booklet, covering the following points:

    - the conditions necessary for a petition for bankruptcy to succeed;
    - the consequences of a petition and a bankruptcy order;
    - the order in which Chancer's debts will be paid;
    - whether Blether Telecom should write this off as a bad debt.

BLETHER TELECOM
BUDGET DATA SHEET

Revenue:

National call (peak)	£0.048 per minute
National call (off-peak)	£0.021 per minute
International call (peak)	£0.105 per minute (average rate)
International call (off-peak)	£0.078 per minute (average rate)

Call volumes (previous three months):

Type of call	Sep. 1997 (minutes)	Oct. 1997 (minutes)	Nov. 1997 (minutes)
National call (peak)	1,195,687	1,203,360	1,231,049
National call (off-peak)	30,651	30,914	31,982
International call (peak)	295,999	296,771	319,754
International call (off-peak)	14,478	14,637	15,980
Total	**1,536,815**	**1,545,682**	**1,598,765**

Projected call mix in the period to March 1998 (based on average over previous 12 months):

Type of call	Percentage share of call volume
National call (peak)	78%
National call (off-peak)	2%
International call (peak)	19%
International call (off-peak)	1%
Total	**100%**

Note: assume call mix will be as above to March 1998.

Projected growth rates (straight-line) in call volumes over the next four months:

Month	Dec	Jan	Feb	Mar
Cumulative Growth rate (%)	2	5	9	11

Assume the mix of call volumes is unchanged.

Direct costs:

Type of call	Cost to Blether Telecom per minute
National call (peak)	0.031
National call (off-peak)	0.014
International call (peak)	0.067
International call (off-peak)	0.050

Overheads:

- Staff costs, £13,350 per month, with a rise of 3.5% in March
- Marketing costs, £5,000 per month. In addition a targeted advertising campaign will be undertaken in the next six months, with costs of £22,000 paid in March
- Other overheads of £9,000 per month are incurred. This includes depreciation of £3,000 per month and a provision for doubtful debts of £200 per month
- Premises costs are paid for by direct debit each month and average £9,350 per month

Other payments:

- A tax bill of £8,500 is payable in December
- Dividend payment of £8,000 is to be paid in March
- Interest is payable on a loan of £275,000 at a rate of 9% p.a., with one year's interest paid in February

Working capital management:

- Customers are billed monthly, with payment being made (on average) 60 days in arrears
- Blether Telecom pays the operating companies supplying the communications monthly, 30 days in arrears
- The cash balance at bank on 31 October 1997 was £51,784

MetalBash plc
EXTRACT FROM REPORT AND ACCOUNTS FOR FOUR YEARS ENDING 31 DECEMBER 1994, 1995, 1996 AND 1997

	1994 £'000	1995 £'000	1996 £'000	1997 £'000
Turnover	5,981,000	6,041,000	6,343,000	6,660,000
Operating expenses (excluding depreciation)	28,700	31,511	33,010	37,384
Earnings before interest and taxation	415,000	284,000	285,500	205,500
Interest charges	76,500	63,472	59,775	79,240
Fixed assets				
Intangible	140,000	160,000	200,000	246,000
Tangible	1,980,000	2,060,000	2,072,000	2,359,000
Investments			20,000	20,000
	2,120,000	2,220,000	2,292,000	2,625,000
Current assets				
Stocks	802,000	864,000	908,000	958,000
Debtors	2,541,000	2,658,000	3,170,000	3,549,000
Cash and short-term investments	90,000	80,000	40,000	10,000
	3,433,000	3,602,000	4,118,000	4,517,000
Current liabilities				
Trade creditors	1,350,000	1,428,000	1,534,000	1,913,000
Bank overdraft	25,000	49,400	549,000	1,008,000
Other			300,000	305,000
	1,375,000	1,477,400	2,383,000	3,226,000
Total assets less current liabilities	4,178,000	4,344,600	4,027,000	3,916,000
Less: loans repayable after more than one year	850,000	744,000	248,000	124,000
Other liabilities	5,000	266,400	319,900	264,400
Net assets	3,323,000	3,334,200	3,459,100	3,527,600
Called up share capital	600,000	600,000	600,000	600,000
Profit and loss account				
Brought forward	2,713,000	2,723,000	2,734,200	2,859,100
Retained for year	10,000	11,200	124,900	68,500
	3,323,000	3,334,200	3,459,100	3,527,600

BLETHER TELECOM AGED DEBTOR ANALYSIS—OCTOBER 1997   Credit Terms: 30 days

Customer name and reference	Total amount	Invoices not yet due	Outstan-ding 1 mth	Outstan-ding 2 mths	Outstan-ding 3 mths	Outstan-ding 3+ mths	Action 1—statement 2—1st reminder 3—2nd reminder 4—telephone call 5—warning letter 6—recovery action implemented					
							1	**2**	**3**	**4**	**5**	**6**
Murray (C003)	12,000	5,000 (Q796)	7,000 (Q749)				3/10 (Q749)					
Calderwood (C102)	6,000		3,000 (Q511)	3,000 (Q423)			3/9 (Q423) 3/10 (Q511)	3/10 (Q423)				
Greenhills (C063)	10,000	2,000 (Q487)			8,000 (Q289)		3/8 (Q289)	3/9 (Q289)	3/10 (Q289)			
Westwood (C098)	1,500					1,500 (Q204)	3/5 (Q204)	3/6 (Q204)	3/7 (Q204)	3/8 (Q204)	3/9 (Q204)	3/10 (Q204)
Hairmyres (C034)	5,500				5,500 (Q334)		3/6 (Q334)	3/7 (Q334)	3/8 (Q334)	3/9 (Q334)	3/10 (Q334)	
Total	35,000	7,000	10,000	3,000	13,500	1,500						

FOULKS*lynch*

BLETHER TELECOM

EXTRACT OF TRANSACTIONS WITH DEBTORS IN NOVEMBER 1997

Customer	Transaction
Murray	Paid invoice Q749 £7,000. Invoice Q796 remains unpaid. Invoice Q721 £5,000 issued.
Calderwood	Paid invoice Q511 £3,000. Invoice Q423 remains unpaid. Invoice Q611 £6,600 issued.
Greenhills	Paid invoice Q487 £2,000. Invoice Q289 remains unpaid. Invoice Q602 £2,775 issued.
Westwood	Invoice Q204 £1,500 remains unpaid. Invoice Q608 issued £4,000.
Hairmyres	Invoice Q334 £2,750 paid.

Customer	Profile
Murray	Medium sized engineering company. Regular customer of 3 years standing. Record of being a good payer.
Calderwood	Independent hotel, 74 employees. Regular customer of 12 months
Greenhills	Large business services subsidiary. Regular customer, but often purchasing from other suppliers.
Westwood	Small retail organisation. Occasional customer of 12 months.
Hairmyres	Medium sized textile group. Once a regular customer. No use of Blether Telecom's facilities for 4 months.

CASH MANAGEMENT AND CREDIT CONTROL

ANSWER BOOKLET

◆ FOULKS*lynch*

ANSWERS (TASK 1)

	Actual Nov	Forecast Dec	Forecast Jan	Forecast Feb	Forecast Mar
Revenue					
National (peak)					
National (off-peak)					
International (peak)					
International (off-peak)					
Subtotal					
Direct costs					
National (peak)					
National (off-peak)					
International (peak)					
International (off-peak)					
Subtotal					
Overheads					
Marketing					
Staff costs					
Other overheads					
Premises					
Taxation					
Dividends					
Interest					
Subtotal					
Net cash flow					
Opening cash flow					
Net cash flow					
Closing cash flow					

Note:	Actual Nov	Forecast Dec	Forecast Jan	Forecast Feb	Forecast Mar
Call volumes (mins)					
TOTAL CALLS					
National (peak)					
National (off-peak)					
International (peak)					
International (off-peak)					

ANSWERS (TASK 2)

ANSWERS (TASK 3)

ANSWERS (TASK 4)

ANSWERS (TASK 5)

ANSWERS (TASK 5, CONTINUED)

ANSWERS (TASK 6)

Relevant data:

	1995 £million	1996 £million	1997 £million
Working capital (net current assets)			
Total assets (fixed and current)			
Debtors, cash and short-term investments			
Daily operating expenses			
Retained earnings (brought forward plus current year)			
Earnings before interest and taxation			
Interest charges plus annual repayment of loans (excluding bank overdraft)			

Ratios expressed in percentages:

	1995 %	1996 %	1997 %
Working capital: total assets			
Retained earnings: total assets			
EBIT: interest charges, plus annual loan repayments			
No credit interval (days)			

ANSWERS (TASK 7)

MEMO

To: Millie Will

From: Jaymini Patel

Subject: MetalBash plc

Date:

ANSWERS (TASK 8)

ANSWERS (TASK 9)

BLETHER TELECOM AGED DEBTOR ANALYSIS—NOVEMBER 1997							Credit Terms: 30 days					
Customer name and reference	Total amount	Invoices not yet due	Outstan -ding 1 mth	Outstan -ding 2 mths	Outstan -ding 3 mths	Outstan -ding 3+ mths	Action 1—statement 2—1st reminder 3—2nd reminder 4—telephone call 5—warning letter 6—recovery action implemented					
							1	2	3	4	5	6
Murray (C003)												
Calderwood (C102)												
Greenhills (C063)												
Westwood (C098)												
Hairmyres (C034)												
Total												

ANSWERS (TASK 9, CONTINUED)

ANSWERS (TASK 9, CONTINUED)

ANSWERS (TASK 10)

ROUGH WORK

CASH MANAGEMENT AND CREDIT CONTROL

SUGGESTED ANSWERS

ANSWERS (TASK 1)

	Actual *Nov*	Forecast *Dec*	Forecast *Jan*	Forecast *Feb*	Forecast *Mar*
Revenue					
National (peak)	57,393	57,761	59,090	61,055	62,851
National (off-peak)	644	649	672	685	705
International (peak)	31,080	31,161	33,574	32,533	33,490
International (off-peak)	1,129	1,142	1,246	1,272	1,309
	90,246	90,713	94,582	95,545	98,355
Direct costs					
National (peak)	37,304	38,163	39,431	40,591	42,137
National (off-peak)	433	448	457	470	488
International (peak)	19,884	21,424	20,759	21,370	22,184
International (off-peak)	732	799	815	839	871
	58,353	60,834	61,462	63,270	65,680
Overheads					
Marketing	5,000	5,000	5,000	5,000	27,000
Staff costs	13,350	13,350	13,350	13,350	13,817
Other overheads	5,800	5,800	5,800	5,800	5,800
Premises	9,350	9,350	9,350	9,350	9,350
Taxation		8,500			
Dividends					8,000
Interest				24,750	
	33,500	42,000	33,500	58,250	63,967
Net cash flow	−1,607	−12,121	−380	−25,975	−31,292
Opening cash flow	51,784	50,177	38,056	37,676	11,701
Net cash flow	−1,607	−12,121	−380	−25,975	−31,292
Closing cash flow	50,177	38,056	37,676	11,701	−19,591

	Actual *Nov*	Forecast *Dec*	Forecast *Jan*	Forecast *Feb*	Forecast *Mar*
Call volumes (mins)					
TOTAL CALLS	1,598,765	1,630,740	1,678,703	1,742,654	1,774,629
National (peak)	1,231,049	1,271,977	1,309,388	1,359,270	1,384,211
National (off-peak)	31,982	32,615	33,574	34,853	35,493
International (peak)	319,754	309,841	318,954	331,104	337,179
International (off-peak)	15,980	16,307	16,787	17,427	17,746

ANSWERS (TASK 2)

The cash surplus in the four months to February 1998 should be invested in an interest-bearing bank deposit account. This should provide easy access to the money and be placed with an institution with an excellent credit rating. Therefore, the emphasis is on safety and liquidity.

The deficit in March 1998 should be funded by a short term credit facility (eg, an overdraft) as it appears to be a short-term requirement.

To improve the cash position, Blether Telecom could:

- consider improving working capital management, which creates a cash requirement, particularly in a fast growing business like Blether Telecom. It could also consider reducing the credit period granted to businesses although this will have an impact on sales;

- consider reducing the rate of growth of the business, perhaps by reducing expenditure on marketing;

- cancel or postpone the dividend payment.

ANSWERS (TASK 3)

Examples might include:

- other capital expenditure (operations manager);
- capital receipts from sale of capital equipment (operations manager);
- share options/rights issues, raising new capital (finance director);
- extraordinary dividend (finance director).

ANSWERS (TASK 4)

To: Douglas Gulland

From: Jaymini Patel

Date: Date of assessment

Subject: Cash forecast

Douglas:

With respect to the cash flow forecast I produced, I suggest:

- November to February—invest cash surplus in safe and liquid investment (eg, bank deposit account)
- March—short-term credit line (eg, overdraft)

It is important to recognise the short-term funding requirement early (ie, at the time of making the forecast) and making arrangements to negotiate a short-term line of credit, in accordance with the organisation's credit procedures on the best possible terms.

Jaymini

ANSWERS (TASK 5)

Introduction

To date, Blether Telecom has been operating using a mix of short and long term funding. However, in the next eighteen months as the growth in our business slows, we will be forecasting a cash surplus. Therefore, a crucial issue will be how this is managed. It is often said, cash is the lifeblood of a business. How cash surpluses are invested is obviously important for the well-being of Blether Telecom.

Key elements of an investment management policy:

The most important considerations when investing cash are:
- safety
- liquidity
- profitability

Safety refers to the likelihood the value of the investment will fall. The liquidity of an investment can be thought of how easily it can be sold and/or converted into cash. The profitability of an investment is the overall return on the investment.

Clearly the most important factor is safety, with the returns on an investment relatively insignificant compared to the actual amount of the investment. Clearly liquidity is very important, if Blether Telecom needs to invest its cash for working capital purposes (ie, pay creditors) or capital (ie, make an acquisition or purchase capital equipment).

Cash investments:

Cash investments are usually deposits in a bank or building society. The essence of cash-based investment is that the security of the capital sum is certain, or as certain as anything can be. Bank deposit accounts go by the name of: deposit accounts, option deposits and so forth. Building society deposits are typically termed: term shares, escalator bonds, notice shares, instant access accounts.

Marketable securities:

Marketable fixed interest securities are types of investments. Their prices are affected by their coupon rate (i.e. the interest rate), the length of time to maturity, the risk associated with the payment of interest and the eventual repayment of capital. Here, UK Government securities are considered (relatively) risk free; but others are not.

ANSWERS (TASK 5, CONTINUED)

EXAMPLES OF MARKETABLE SECURITIES

UK Government securities Also known as gilts, and form the largest part of the 'fixed interest' market. Gilts are usually classified by their maturity (eg, shorts—up to 5 years, longs—over 15 years etc.). A limited number of variable rate, index-linked and convertible gilts are also available.

Commercial paper The term for certificates issued by a company promising to pay an amount to the person bearing the note on a specified date. Commercial paper is an unsecured borrowing issued for a short period of time usually no more than one year (and often less).

Debentures Similar to commercial paper, being debt stock issued by a company. However, debentures are usually secured on a particular asset and the loan is for a long term (i.e. usually five or ten years).

Certificates of Deposit are issued by institutions and are negotiable instruments certifying that a sum has been deposited with the issuer (a bank or building society) to be repaid on a certain date. The term can vary from 7 days to up to 5 years.

Bills of exchange are similar to cheques. Examples of bills of exchange include: term bills (short term with a maturity from two weeks to six months), trade bills (drawn by one non-bank company on another company) and bankers' acceptances (drawn by a bank).

Summary: an outline policy for Blether Telecom

When considering investing cash due consideration should be given to the following (in descending order) the safety of the investment, its liquidity and the return on the investment.

- To manage risk, limits should be in place to ensure cash is invested in a spread of marketable securities, leaving no exposure to a particular market or instrument.
- Credit ratings should be employed, so for example, Blether Telecom should invest in securities rated AA (long term) or A+ (short-term).
- Overnight cash surpluses should be invested in a cash deposit account, with surpluses expected say, over a month, invested in a marketable security (of assessed credit quality) to gain a better return.
- All investments should be reviewed by senior management every month.

ANSWERS (TASK 6)

Relevant data

	1995 £million	1996 £million	1997 £million
Working capital (net current assets)	2,124.6	1,735.0	1,291.0
Total assets (fixed and current)	5,822.0	6,410.0	7,142.0
Debtors, cash and short-term investments	2,738.0	3,210.0	3,559.0
Daily operating expenses	86.332	90.438	102.422
Retained earnings (brought forward plus current year)	2,734.2	2,859.1	2,927.6
Earnings before interest and taxation	284.0	285.5	205.5
Interest charges plus annual repayment of loans (excluding bank overdraft)	169.472	555.775	203.24

Ratios expressed in percentages

	1995 %	1996 %	1997 %
Working capital: total assets	36.49	27.07	18.08
Retained earnings: total assets	46.96	44.60	40.99
EBIT: interest charges plus annual loan repayments	167.58	51.37	101.11
No credit interval (days)	31.71	35.49	34.75

ANSWERS (TASK 7)

MEMO

To: Millie Will

From: Jaymini Patel

Subject: MetalBash plc

Date:

Purpose of the ratios

The working capital: total assets ratio identifies the business's investment in working capital as a proportion of total assets. A high ratio indicates excessive investment in working capital, whilst a very low ratio could suggest a lack of liquidity caused by overtrading.

The no credit ratio shows the number of days an organisation could survive, by paying its regular, day-to-day expenses from cash and short-term investments. It indicates liquidity and the safety margin which a business has.

The retained earnings: total assets ratio shows the retained earnings as a proportion of total assets. Usually this figure would be quite high as an organisation with substantial fixed assets will need significant capital to maintain them, use them effectively and replace them.

The earnings before interest and taxation: interest charge plus annual repayment of loans ratio indicates a company's ability to meet its obligations to lenders. Typically, earnings need to be significantly higher than those obligations (perhaps by a factor of two or three) to ensure that the organisation can survive a temporary fall in earnings.

Trends in ratios

Working capital has fallen over the period, both in absolute terms (pounds) and relative terms (percentages). This is mainly due to a growth in current liabilities, most noticeably the bank overdraft.

The no credit interval period rose between 1995 and 1996, and deteriorated slightly in 1997.

The fall in retained earnings as a proportion of total assets over the past two years, despite the increase in retained earnings, suggest the dividend policy is too generous for a company with rapidly growing assets.

Earnings did not cover interest charges and loan repayments in 1996 and only just in 1997. This may explain the company replacing long-term credit with short-term debt. However, this ratio improved dramatically in 1997 indicating this position may soon (favourably) reverse.

Conclusion

On the evidence supplied by the historic accounts, MetalBash is not a good credit risk. Blether Telecom should not grant credit to MetalBash. Trading with MetalBash should only be conducted if MetalBash can provide some additional form of guarantee, perhaps from their bank, and should be for a reduced credit period.

ANSWERS (TASK 8)

It is important to:
- convey that Blether Telecom are not prepared to trade on credit at present, but that they are willing to trade if a suitable guarantee is provided;
- that the situation can be reviewed in the future;
- that this is communicated in a firm yet polite manner, regardless of MetalBash's reaction.

ANSWERS (TASK 9)

BLETHER TELECOM AGED DEBTOR ANALYSIS—NOVEMBER 1997							Credit Terms: 30 days					
Customer name and reference	Total amount	Invoices not yet due	Outstan -ding 1 mth	Outstan -ding 2 mths	Outstan -ding 3 mths	Outstan -ding 3+ mths	Action 1—statement 2—1st reminder 3—2nd reminder 4—telephone call 5—warning letter 6—recovery action implemented					
							1	**2**	**3**	**4**	**5**	**6**
Murray (C003)	10,000	5,000 (Q721)	5,000 (Q796)				3/11 (Q796)					
Calderwood (C102)	9,600	6,600 (Q611)			3,000 (Q423)		3/9 (Q423) 3/10 (Q511)	3/11 (Q423)				
Greenhills (C063)	10,775	2,775 (Q602)				8,000 (Q289)	3/8 (Q289)	3/9 (Q289)	3/11 (Q289)			
Westwood (C098)	5,500	4,000 (Q608)				1,500 (Q204)	3/5 (Q204)	3/6 (Q204)	3/7 (Q204)	3/8 (Q204)	3/9 (Q204)	3/10 (Q204)
Hairmyres (C034)	2,750					2,750 (Q334)	3/6 (Q334)	3/7 (Q334)	3/8 (Q334)	3/9 (Q334)	3/10 (Q334)	
Total	38,625	18,375	5,000	0	3,000	12,250						

ANSWERS (TASK 9, CONTINUED)

Murray (C003)

Murray is a regular payer and has one outstanding debt. The required action is to send Murray its regular statement. No further action.

Calderwood (C102)

Calderwood has one invoice now outstanding for three months. Although the required action indicates a second reminder, perhaps a telephone call would also be useful given the indication that Calderwood is an irregular payer.

Greenhills (C063)

This customer has one invoice outstanding over 3+ months. As Greenhills has been a regular customer this suggests there is a problem with the invoice, possibly relating to a quality or service issue. A visit to the customer is recommended before legal action is taken. Consider treating as a bad debt.

Westwood (C098)

Westwood has an invoice long overdue. However, Blether Telecom is still trading with the customer, indicating a problem with its credit function. No further credit should be allowed to Westwood. Blether Telecom should attempt to contact Westwood to ascertain the problem. If a satisfactory answer cannot be found, recovery action should be instigated. Consider treating as a bad debt.

Hairmyres (C034)

Hairmyres has now paid half of its long overdue account. Before proceeding to take court action to recover the remaining amount due Blether Telecom should establish whether a dispute exists with the customer, and their credit status.

ANSWERS (TASK 10)

NOTES

Three weeks after we have served the debtor (John Chancer) with a statutory demand, we can petition the court for a bankruptcy order.

For a bankruptcy order to succeed:
- the debt must be in excess of £750;
- the debt must be unsecured;
- the debtor must be domiciled in England and Wales.

However, if the statutory demand has been complied with or there is a reasonable prospect of Chancer paying the debt, the petition will be dismissed.

The consequences of a petition are:
- if Chancer pays money to creditors or disposes of property, these transactions are void;
- any other legal proceedings relating to the debtor's property or debts are suspended;
- an interim receiver is appointed, to protect the estate (by selling goods that may diminish in value).

The consequences of a bankruptcy order are:
- the official receiver takes control of Chancer's property;
- a statement of Chancer's assets and liabilities is drawn up (a statement of affairs);
- the receiver summons a meeting of creditors, within 12 weeks of the bankruptcy order;
- the creditors appoint a trustee in bankruptcy;
- Chancer's assets are realised and a distribution of these assets made to the creditors.

Different types of creditors are paid in a certain order. These different claims are ranked in order:

1. fees paid by an apprentice or articled clerks training;
2. preferential creditors such as: Inland Revenue for PAYE; subcontractors in the building industry; Customs and Excise for VAT; car tax and other excise duties; national insurance contributions; pension scheme contributions; employees' wages for four months up to £800;
3. ordinary creditors.

The consequence is that if Blether Telecom do successfully petition for Chancer to be made bankrupt, they may be placed towards the back of the queue when the receiver distributes what is left of Chancer's assets. That the debt has been outstanding for such a period and that Blether Telecom are considering such severe action indicates that they should treat this as a bad debt for accounting purposes.

SECTION D

COVERAGE OF PERFORMANCE CRITERIA

The following performance criteria are covered in this simulation. An indication of which performance criteria are covered by the individual tasks is given in brackets following the task assessment criteria (see page 38).

Element	PC Coverage
14.1 (ii) (iii) (iv) (v)	**Monitor and control cash receipts and payments** • Appropriate staff are consulted to determine the likely pattern of cash flows over the accounting period and to anticipate any exceptional receipts or payments • Forecasts of future cash payments and receipts are in accord with known income and expenditure trends • Cash budgets are prepared in the approved format and clearly indicate net cash requirements • Significant deviations from the cash budget are identified and corrective action is taken within defined organisational policies
14.2 (i) (ii) (iii) (iv) (v)	**Manage cash balances** • Overdraft and loan facilities are arranged in anticipation of requirements and on the most favourable terms available • Surplus funds are invested in marketable securities within defined financial authorisation limits • The organisation's financial regulations and security procedures are observed • Account is taken of trends in the economic and financial environment in managing cash balances • An adequate level of liquidity is maintained in line with cash forecasts
14.3 (i) (ii) (iii) (iv)	**Grant credit** • Credit terms are agreed with customers in accordance with the organisation's policies • Internal and external sources of information are identified and used to evaluate the current credit status of customers and potential customers • New accounts are opened for those customers with an established credit status • The reasons for refusing credit are discussed with customers in a tactful manner
14.4 (i) (ii) (iii) (iv) (v)	**Monitor and control the collection of debts** • Information relating to the current state of debtors' accounts is regularly monitored and appropriate action taken • Information regarding significant outstanding accounts and potential bad debts is promptly sent to relevant individuals within the organisation • Discussions and negotiations with debtors are conducted courteously and achieve the desired outcome • Debt recovery methods used are appropriate to the circumstances of individual cases and are in accordance with the organisation's procedures • Recommendations to write off bad and doubtful debts are based on a realistic analysis of all known factors

The following performance criterion from element 14.1(14.1(i)) is not covered in this simulation and should be separately assessed.

• Cash receipts and payments are monitored and controlled against budgeted cash flow.

ASSESSMENT CRITERIA

Assessors must refer to the Standards of Competence for Accounting and be guided by the performance criteria when evaluating candidates' work.

Task 1   Candidates should make no more than eight errors. (14.1 (iii), 14.1 (iv))

Task 2   Candidates should recognise the cash position in the cash flow forecast they have produced and suggest a suitable means for investing and borrowing the cash. Candidates should also identify at least TWO appropriate means of improving cash flow. Delaying payments to creditors is not regarded as an acceptable practice. (14.1(v))

Task 3   Candidates should identify at least TWO appropriate items along with a suitable individual in the organisation. It is realised that this individual will vary considerably in different organisations. (14.1 (ii))

Task 4   Candidates should identify the need to invest cash in a secure and liquid investment and the need to negotiate a line of credit (if this has not already been done). (14.2 (i))

Task 5   For candidates to be assessed as competent the presentation should cover all points briefly. (14.2 (ii) – (v))

Task 6   *One error* of arithmetic will be allowed. (14.3 (ii))

Task 7   The commentary should make brief but appropriate comments for all four ratios. This should be communicated clearly. (14.3 (i), 14.3 (ii), 14.3 (iii))

Task 8   The response should emphasise two things: the limitation of not being able to grant credit (or alternatively with restrictions) and that this should be communicated in a polite and diplomatic fashion. (14.3 (iv))

Task 9   Candidates may make up to *two errors* in completing the analysis. Actions suggested should be appropriate to the account and not overly heavy-handed. (14.4 (i)—(iii))

Task 10   Only an outline understanding of the mechanics and effects of bankruptcy is expected. Candidates should display at least some background knowledge. Candidates should also identify this as a potential bad debt. (14.4 (iv), 14.4 (v))

Overall assessment

Candidates may be allowed to make further minor errors, providing such errors do not suggest a fundamental lack of understanding.

Candidates must not be penalised more than once for an error. If a candidate transfers an incorrect figure to another part of the exercise, this is not counted as a further error.

General
- It is expected that work will be neatly and competently presented
- Pencil will not be accepted
- Liquid correcting fluid may be used but it should be used in moderation.

Discretion

In having regard to the above criteria, the assessor is entitled in marginal cases to exercise discretion in the candidate's favour. Such discretion shall only be exercised where other criteria are met to above the required standard and, in the opinion of the assessor, the assessment overall demonstrates competence and would be of an acceptable standard in the workplace.

QUESTIONS

1–2   CASHFLOW AND CASH BUDGETS

1   Activity

The following data and estimates are available for ABC Ltd for June, July and August:

	June £	July £	August £
Sales	45,000	50,000	60,000
Wages	12,000	13,000	14,500
Overheads	8,500	9,500	9,000

The following information is available regarding direct materials:

	June £	July £	August £	September £
Opening stock	5,000	3,500	6,000	4,000
Material usage	8,000	9,000	10,000	
Closing stock	3,500	6,000	4,000	

Notes:

(1)   10% of sales are for cash, the balance is received the following month. The amount received in June for May's sales is £29,500.

(2)   Wages are paid in the month they are incurred.

(3)   Overheads include £1,500 per month for depreciation. Overheads are settled the month following. £6,500 is to be paid in June for May's overheads.

(4)   Purchases of direct materials are paid for in the month purchased.

(5)   The opening cash balance in June is £11,750.

(6)   A tax bill of £25,000 is to be paid in July.

Task

(a)   Calculate the amount of direct material purchases in EACH of the months of June, July and August.

(b)   Prepare cash budgets for June, July and August.

(c)   Describe briefly the advantages of preparing cash budgets.

2   Activity

B Ltd makes and sells a single product, the standard cost and selling price data of which are shown below for 2003:

		£
5 kg of raw material	@ £3.00 per kg	15.00
2 hours labour	@ £4.50 per hour	9.00
Variable overhead	@ £2.00 per hour	4.00
Fixed overhead	@ £4.00 per hour	8.00
		36.00
Profit		14.00
Selling price		50.00

The budgeted sales for the first four accounting periods of 2003 are:

January	5,000 units
February	4,000 units
March	6,000 units
April	8,000 units

Finished stocks are expected to be 2,500 units at the beginning of January 2003. The budget should be prepared on the basis that stocks at the beginning of each month are required to be equal to 50% of that month's budgeted sales.

The fixed overhead cost per unit shown in the standard cost data is based on the annual labour budget for 2003 of 144,000 hours. Annual depreciation of £57,600 is included in the fixed overhead cost.

Raw materials are paid for one month after they are used in production. B Ltd does not keep any raw material stocks.

Labour costs are paid in the month in which the costs are incurred.

50% of the total overhead payable is paid in the month in which the cost is incurred, the remainder is paid in the following month.

25% of the sales are cash sales, the remainder are on credit. An analysis of the past credit sales indicates that:

60% are paid in the month after sale
30% are paid two months after sale
and the remainder are bad debts

The following balances are expected at the beginning of January 2003:

			£
Bank balance			3,000
Creditors	-	Materials	30,000
	-	Overhead	31,500
Debtors	-	December 2002 sales	75,000
	-	November 2002 sales	30,000

Task

(a)   Prepare B Ltd's production budget for the first three months of 2003, showing clearly the number of units to be produced in each period;

(b)   Prepare B Ltd's cash budget for the first three months of 2003, showing clearly the projected bank balance at the end of each month.

◈ **FOULKS**lynch

3   Activity

A wholesale company ends its financial year on 30 June. You have been requested, in early July 2003, to assist in the preparation of a cash forecast. The following information is available regarding the company's operations:

(a)   Management believes that the 2002/2003 sales level and pattern are a reasonable estimate of 2003/2004 sales. Sales in 2002/2003 were as follows:

		£
2002	July	360,000
	August	420,000
	September	600,000
	October	540,000
	November	480,000
	December	400,000
2003	January	350,000
	February	550,000
	March	500,000
	April	400,000
	May	600,000
	June	800,000
	Total	6,000,000

(b)   The accounts receivable at 30 June 2003 total £380,000. Sales collections are generally made as follows:

During month of sale	60%
In first subsequent month	30%
In second subsequent month	9%
Uncollectable	1%

(c)   The purchase cost of goods averages 60% of selling price. The cost of the stock on hand at 30 June 2003 is £840,000, of which £30,000 is obsolete. Arrangements have been made to sell the obsolete stock in July at half the normal selling price on a cash on delivery basis. The company wishes to maintain the stock, as of the first of each month, at a level of three months' sales as determined by the sales forecast for the next three months. All purchases are paid for on the tenth of the following month. Accounts payable for purchases at 30 June 200X total £370,000.

(d)   Payments in respect of fixed and variable expenses are forecast for the first three months of 2003/2004 as follows:

	£
July	160,620
August	118,800
September	158,400

(e)   It is anticipated that cash dividends of £40,000 will be paid each half year, on the fifteenth day of September and March.

(f)   During the year unusual advertising costs will be incurred that will require cash payments of £10,000 in August and £15,000 in September. The advertising costs are in addition to the expenses in item (d) above.

(g)   Equipment replacements are made at a rate which requires a cash outlay of £3,000 per month. The equipment has an average estimated life of six years.

(h)   A £60,000 payment for corporation tax is to be made on 15 September 2003.

(i)   At 30 June 2003 the company had a bank loan with an unpaid balance of £280,000. The entire balance is due on 30 September 2003, together with accumulated interest from 1 July 2003 at the rate of 12% pa.

(j)   The cash balance at 30 June 2003 is £100,000.

Task

Prepare a cash forecast statement, by months, for the first three months of the 2003/2004 financial year. The statement should show the amount of cash on hand (or deficiency of cash) at the end of each month. All computations and supporting schedules should be presented in clear and concise form.

4   Activity

From the following statements, prepare a month-by-month cash budget for the six months to 31 December.

(a)   **Revenue budget (ie, trading and profit and loss account)**

Six months to 31 December (all revenue/costs accrue evenly over the six months)

	£'000	£'000
Sales (cash received one month in arrear)		1,200
Cost of sales:		
Paid one month in arrear	900	
Paid in month of purchase	144	
Depreciation	72	
		1,116
Budgeted profit		84

(b)   **Capital budget**

	£'000	£'000
Payments for new plant:		
July	12	
August	25	
September	13	
November	50	
		100
Increase in stocks, payable August		20
		120
Receipts:		
New issue of share capital (October)		30

(c)   **Balance sheet**

	Actual 1 July £'000
Assets side:	
Fixed assets	720
Stocks	100
Debtors	210
Cash	40
	1,070
Liabilities side:	
Capital and reserves	856
Taxation (payable December)	30
Creditors - trade	160
Dividends (payable August)	24
	1,070

5 Activity

XYZ Ltd has the following forecast sales at list price for the nine months to 29 February 2002:

June	£40,000	September	£48,000	December	£44,000
July	£44,000	October	£40,000	January	£42,000
August	£50,000	November	£45,000	February	£50,000

60% of the company's sales are on credit, payable in the month after sale. Cash sales attract a 5% discount off list price.

Purchases amount to 40% of selling price, and these are paid for two months after delivery.

Stock is maintained at a level equal to 50% of the following month's sales except that in November stock is to be increased by £2,000 (at cost prices) to ensure that XYZ Ltd has a safety stock during the period when its major supplier shuts down. This safety stock will be released in March.

Wages comprise a fixed sum of £2,000 per month plus a variable element equal to 10% of sales; these are payable in the month they are incurred.

Fixed costs amount to £7,500 per month, payable one month in arrears, of which £1,500 is depreciation.

XYZ Ltd has capital expenditure/receipts scheduled as follows:

Acquisitions:	£
September	15,000
November	10,000
February	4,000
Disposal:	
October	8,000

Corporation tax, payable in November, amounts to £44,000.

The bank balance on 1 September 200X is expected to be £5,000.

Task

(a)   Prepare a cashflow forecast for XYZ Ltd for EACH of the six months from September 2001 to February 2002, using a row and column format.

(b)   Explain clearly, using your answer to (a) above, how a spreadsheet may be used to assist in the preparation of cash forecasts.

3   FORECASTING TECHNIQUES

1   Activity

The managers of a company are preparing revenue plans for the last quarter of Year 4, and for the first three quarters of Year 5. The data below refer to one of the main products:

Revenue	April–June Quarter 1 £'000	July–September Quarter 2 £'000	October–December Quarter 3 £'000	January–March Quarter 4 £'000
Year 1	49	37	58	67
Year 2	50	38	59	68
Year 3	51	40	60	70
Year 4	50	42	61	-

Task

(a)   Calculate the four-quarterly moving average trend for this set of data.

(b)   calculate the seasonal factors.

2   Activity

The following table shows data for gross domestic product (GDP), gross earnings and retail prices for the UK, Years 1-10:

Year	Gross domestic product (market prices, £ billion)	Average gross earnings (Year 6 = 100)	Retail prices (Year 6 = 100)
1	231	65	71
2	255	73	79
3	278	80	86
4	303	87	90
5	323	92	94
6	354	100	100
7	379	108	103
8	414	116	108
9	430	126	113
10	436*	136*	122*

* provisional

Task

(a)   Convert the GDP series to index numbers with Year 6 = 100.

(b)   Calculate deflated index numbers for GDP and average gross earnings, with Year 6 = 100.

(c)   Plot the two deflated indicators against time on the same graph and to comment critically upon the meaning of these data.

4-5   THE ECONOMY AND BANKS

1   Activity

Your business has an overdraft with the South East Bank. In this relationship between your business and the bank who is the debtor and who is the creditor?

2   Activity

Arthur has £130 remaining in his bank current account and no agreed overdraft facility. He has just written a cheque for £150 (with no supporting cheque guarantee card).

Task

Briefly describe the bank's options regarding this cheque.

3   Activity

Consider the cheque given below:

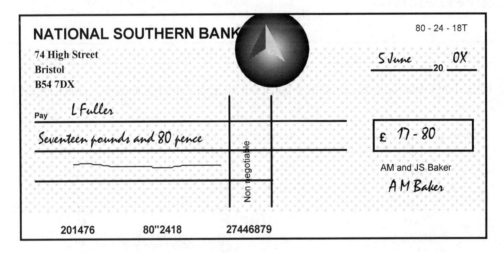

Task

Name each of the following parties to the cheque:

(a)   the drawer;
(b)   the drawee;
(c)   the payee.

4   Activity

Consider the cheques reproduced below.

Task

List any errors that can be found on the cheques.

(a)   **Front:**

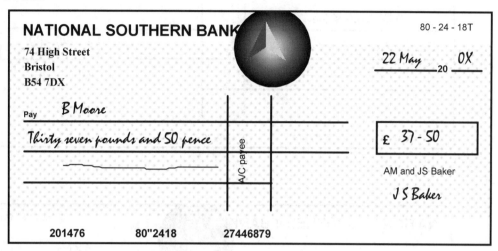

Back:

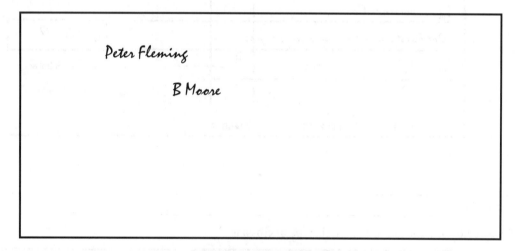

(b)

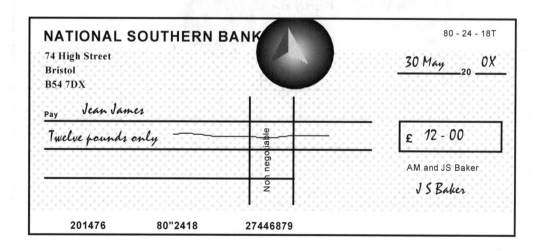

(c)

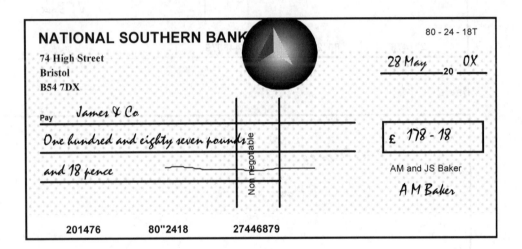

(d)

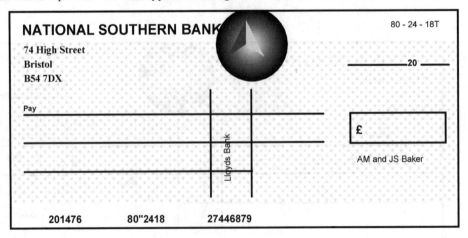

5   Activity

Given below is a cheque with a certain type of crossing.

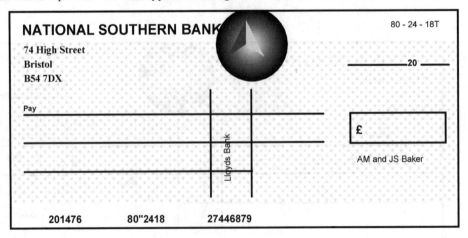

Task

State the name given to this type of crossing and briefly explain its effect.

6   Activity

You are a new till assistant in a supermarket. Produce a brief checklist that you can keep by your till indicating the items that you should check before accepting a cheque as payment.

7   Activity

Phil wishes to purchase an item that costs £160. His cheque guarantee card is for £100. He suggests to the seller that he writes out one cheque for £100 and another for £60.

Task

Explain whether the seller would be wise to accept this form of payment if:

(a)   Phil intends to take the goods away immediately;

(b)   It is agreed that the seller will deliver the goods in one weeks time.

8   Activity

Two weeks ago you banked a cheque from a credit customer, Jones Ltd. The bank has now returned the cheque to you marked "Refer to Drawer".

Task

Explain what is usually meant by such an endorsement.

6-8   TREASURY AND RAISING FINANCE

1   Activity

(a)   Identify the major financial intermediaries in the UK.

(b)   Why does a modern economy require financial intermediaries?

2   Activity

Describe the ways in which a public limited company may finance its activities.

3   Activity

Explain briefly how stock markets work and assess their usefulness to business as a source of long-term capital.

4   Activity

Data

You have recently been appointed to a position in the cash management section of the accounting department at Stenwater Limited, a marine construction contracting company based in Aberdeen. The company was formed by the merger of two local companies eighteen months ago and it has been experiencing some administrative difficulties following the rapid expansion of business.

From your work so far, you are aware that Stenwater's procedures for managing the cash collection process are rather basic and some improvements could be made.

You have already identified some of the symptoms of poor cash management. These are addressed by assessment tasks 1 to 4.

Task 1

No procedures exist to ensure that delays do not occur in the company's internal handling procedures. Suggest ONE way in which funds could be delayed within Stenwater before they are paid into the bank.

Task 2

Most customers pay directly to Stenwater's bankers by either Telegraphic Transfer or BACS. What payment instructions must you send to these customers?

Suggest FIVE items.

Task 3

There is little communication with the debtor. Identify TWO ways in which the collection process might be assisted if you kept in contact with the appropriate individual in the cash management section of the paying company.

Task 4

No system exists to receive bank balances, other than weekly bank statements supplied by the bank. Why is it important that daily balances are received?

5   Activity

Task 1

Briefly describe what is meant by the term 'marketable security'.

Task 2

Give TWO examples of a marketable security used in liquidity management.

Task 3

A key feature of a bank overdraft is the uncommitted nature of the funds.
When can a bank ask for such a facility to be repaid?

6   Activity

According to the Institute of Chartered Accountants in England and Wales, the benefits of good cash management to a company are:

- better control of financial risk
- opportunity for profit
- strengthened balance sheet
- increased confidence with customers, suppliers, banks and shareholders.

Explain how good cash management may realise EACH of these benefits.

(a)   Better control of financial risk
(b)   Opportunity for profit
(c)   Strengthened balance sheet
(d)   Increased confidence with customers, suppliers, banks and shareholders

7   Activity

Debt factoring and invoice discounting are both ways of raising short-term finance. Describe TWO ways in which they differ.

8   Activity

An important method of finance provided by the UK banking system is the overdraft. List THREE features of an overdraft facility.

9 BASIC LAW OF CONTRACT

1 Activity

Explain the following rules in relation to the formation of a contract and identify any exceptions to them.

(a) Consideration must exist and have value but need not be adequate.

(b) Consideration may be present or future but must not be past.

(c) A promise to perform an existing obligation may not be consideration.

2 Activity

Explain, with reasons, whether a valid contract has been formed between Sidney and Brian in each of the following situations.

(a) Sidney agrees to sell goods to Brian 'on the usual terms'.

(b) Sidney offers to sell goods to Brian for £500. Brian says he will pay £400 but Sidney refuses to reduce his price. Brian then says he will pay £500.

(c) Sidney agrees to deliver goods to Brian on the condition that Tom pays him £200.

(d) Sidney offers to sell goods to Brian and gives him ten days to decide whether he wishes to buy them. After five days Sidney sells the goods elsewhere. Two days later, Brian says that he accepts the offer.

3 Activity

Nigel offered to sell his car to Georgina for £3,000. Georgina said that she would like to buy the car, and would pay half the amount immediately, and the remaining £1,500 at the end of the following month. Georgina did nothing for three days, but then heard that Nigel had sold the car for £2,800 to Martin.

(a) Has Georgina got a binding contract with Nigel?

(b) Briefly explain the reason for your answer.

4 Activity

James offered by fax to buy his friend Jonathan's CD player for £200, and ended the message by writing 'I'll assume it's mine if I hear no more'. James was then annoyed to discover that after Jonathan had received the fax, he had sold the CD player to Annabel.

(a) Does James' offer to Jonathan give rise to a binding contract between them?

(b) Briefly explain the reason for your answer.

5   Activity

Michael said that he would give Lucy, his next door neighbour, his old computer and printer, as Michael had just bought a new computer system. When Lucy went round to Michael's house to collect the goods, Michael told her that he had changed his mind and was going to sell them through the local newspaper.

(a)   Can Lucy force Michael to honour his promise and give her the goods?

(b)   Briefly explain the reason for your answer.

6   Activity

Mark bought a car from Tim, who had advertised it for sale in the local newspaper. Unbeknown to either of them, it had been stolen from Henry some months previously, and then sold on to Tim.

What are Mark's rights in this situation?

10   GRANTING CREDIT

1   Activity

You are in the process of arranging the granting of credit to a potential customer. As part of this process you are preparing a detailed ratio analysis based on that company's last three years' annual accounts. You prepare a similar analysis for every new customer the company does business with. Suggest THREE reasons why such an analysis may be helpful.

2   Activity

In gathering credit information on a potential client, identify TWO sources of internal credit information and TWO sources of external information.

3   Activity

Fidelity Computers regularly runs credit checks on new customers by using Credit Check Ltd, a credit reference agency. Such agencies are excluded from the Data Protection Act.

Is Credit Check Ltd obliged to allow a sole trader access to data held on its computers?

4   Activity

Stoneybridge Limited has trade debtors at the end of November 200X of £52,000. Average daily credit sales are £2,500. Calculate the debtor collection period in days.

11   MONITORING AND CONTROL

1   Activity

Data

You have recently joined the accounting department of Barnaby Soft Drinks Limited as an Accounting Technician. Barnaby is a family-owned business based in New Cross, South East London. It has traded now for fourteen years and produces a range of still and fizzy drinks which it markets from a range of retail outlets it owns in the capital. The soft drinks sector is noted for providing its shareholders with a steady cash flow and stable profits.

Recently, Barnaby has signed agreements with a number of distributors to market its products nationwide. But, since signing these agreements, Barnaby's cash flow has been affected because these credit sales now represent 35% of its turnover (as opposed to 5% before the new marketing agreements). The remainder of its sales are cash sales to customers at its own retail outlets.

Barnaby has operated successfully without a formal credit policy or credit control function since the start of trading. Its new marketing strategy has provided good growth and improved profitability. However, the Finance Director has recently had to negotiate an extended overdraft facility and is concerned that the latest cash flow forecast has many associated uncertainties. Some of Barnaby's larger customers have been taking over 80 days (as opposed to 30 days according to the terms of sale) to settle their accounts.

Task 1

What is meant by the term ´credit policy`?

Task 2

Using the headed paper which follows, outline in a brief memorandum to the Finance Director the key features that should be contained in a credit policy.

BARNABY SOFT DRINKS LIMITED

MEMORANDUM

To: Finance Director

From: Accounting Technician

Date: 13 December 200X

Subject: Credit Control Policy

Task 3

To cope with the additional volume of sales, Barnaby has invested in a new sales accounting system. Every month (and as required) an Aged Analysis of Debtors Report will be produced, itemised by customer. The consultants installing the system have asked what you would like to see from such a report.

Design a suitable report below.

BARNABY SOFT DRINKS LIMITED

AGED ANALYSIS OF DEBTORS

Task 4

The Finance Director has heard that a lot of collection delays relate to customer queries.

How might customer queries cause difficulties when collecting amounts due from trade debtors?

Task 5

Describe TWO features that are desirable in a policy of managing customer queries.

2	Activity

Collection agencies exist to assist companies with collecting debts. Typically a commercial agency will charge a proportion of the debt collected, with no charge if no collection is made.

When approaching a credit collection agency, what points would you look for from such an agency? List THREE items.

PRACTICE ASSESSMENT ACTIVITIES

QUESTIONS

Note: Until recently this unit was centrally assessed. You will find the following activities useful for practice purposes.

◈ FOULKS*lynch*

CASH MANAGEMENT AND CREDIT CONTROL
(PREVIOUSLY UNIT 9 AND UNIT 14)

QUESTIONS

JUNE 1996

This central assessment is in THREE sections. You are reminded that competence must be achieved in each section. You should therefore aim to complete EVERY task in EACH section. Write your answers in the spaces provided.

You are advised to spend approximately 1 hour on Section 1, 1 hour 10 minutes on Section 2 and 50 minutes on Section 3.

Note: Any essential calculations should be included within your answer where appropriate.

SECTION 1

Data

Greenock Belting PLC is a company whose main activity is the manufacture of synthetic fabric for the engineering industry. The Cash Manager is preparing an analysis of the company's cash flow. The company's overdraft at the start of the financial year, 1 July 1996, is expected to be £1,773,000. Greenock Belting's expected final profit and loss account for the year ending 30 June 1996 is shown on the next page.

Greenock Belting PLC: Profit and loss account and notes for the year ending 30 June 1996

		£'000	Note
Sales		12,790	
Less:	Wages	3,125	
	Raw materials and components	4,800	
	Production overheads	2,865	
	Depreciation	1,375	
	Other expenses	300	1
Operating profit		325	
Interest charged		75	2
Other income		325	3
TOTAL NET PROFIT		575	

Notes [1] The item includes £200,000 of research expenditure. Additionally, development expenditure of £125,000 has been deferred and capitalised and will be carried forward to begin writing off in 1999.

[2] In addition to the amount charged in the profit and loss account, interest of £125,000 has been capitalised representing intangible assets.

[3] Other income refers to the company's share in the earnings of associate undertakings. In the year ended 30 June 1996, the company actually received cheques for £100,000 from associates in dividends.

Assumptions

The following assumptions have been established to forecast cash flow for the year ending 30 June 1997:

Sales are forecast to increase by 10%.

The **depreciation charge** is forecast as £1.4 million. **Capital expenditure** is expected to be £1.5 million.

Wages The total hours worked will remain the same and wages to increase by 5%.

Production overheads These are expected to increase in value by 4% p.a.

Raw materials and components These are expected to increase in value by 8%.

Interest and other income and other expenses are expected to remain unchanged.

Credit terms Greenock's trade debtors take on average three months to pay while it is company policy to take two months' credit from suppliers of raw materials and components. All wages are paid at the end of each month, and on average 8% of production overheads remain unpaid at the end of the year to which they relate.

Task 1

You are required to:

(a)   forecast the company's profit and loss account for the year ending 30 June 1997; and

(b)   forecast their cash flow position for the year ending 30 June 1997, using Greenock's pro-forma budget form below.

GREENOCK BELTING PLC
1997 BUDGET
DATE OF REPORT: ....

Forecast profit and loss account for the year ending 30 June 1997

	£'000
Sales	
Less: Wages	
Raw materials and components	
Production overheads	
Depreciation	
Other expenses	
Operating profit	
Interest charged	
Other income	
TOTAL NET PROFIT	

Cash flow forecast for the year ending 30 June 1997

	£'000
Operating profit	
Depreciation	
(Increase) in trade debtors	
Increase in trade creditors	
Production overheads	
Operating cash flow	
Interest paid	
Development expenditure	
Capital expenditure	
Dividends	
Net cash flow	
Opening cash position	
Net cash flow	
Closing cash position	

Task 2

Identify FIVE sources of uncertainty in Greenock's forecast cash flow.

....

....

....

....

....

....

....

....

....

....

SECTION 2

Task 1

You are employed as a Credit Controller in a national telecommunications company. The Chief Accountant has heard about credit insurance at a conference and has asked your advice on it. Your advice should be in the form of a memorandum and should describe the different types of cover available and why companies may choose to use it.

Use the memorandum sheet on the following page for your answer.

MEMORANDUM

To: Chief Accountant

From: Credit Controller

Date:

Subject: Uses of Credit Insurance

_____

_____

_____

_____

_____

_____

_____

_____

_____

_____

_____

_____

_____

_____

_____

_____

_____

_____

_____

_____

_____

Task 2

(a)   What is the main drawback associated with using published reports and accounts for credit control information?

....

....

....

....

....

(b)   A company is insolvent when it cannot pay its debts as they fall due. Identify **TWO** routes for a creditor to recover bad debts and briefly describe what is involved.

....

....

....

....

....

....

(c)   Using the courts to recover bad debts is costly and time consuming. Describe **THREE** methods of enforcing a judgement in the county courts.

....

....

....

....

....

....

....

....

....

....

SECTION 3

Task 1

In a banking context, what is a CD? Describe **THREE** of its characteristics.

....

....

....

....

....

Task 2

What is meant by the term 'Data Subject' in the Data Protection Act 1984?

....

....

Task 3

When managing an organisation's cash flow, what does a cashier understand by the term 'cleared funds'?

....

....

Task 4

(a)   For many small companies, factoring proves an attractive alternative to bank lending. Typically, bank lenders are concerned with the state of a company's balance sheet. What element of a company's balance sheet do factors consider when advancing funds?

....

....

(b)   Factoring and discounting have experienced steady growth in recent years: 20 per cent compound growth each year since 1981.

List **THREE** services provided by factors and discounters.

....

....

....

....

....

Task 5

Read the following two scenarios. In each case, in your role as Cash Manager, advise the Finance Director what type of bank borrowing would be most suitable and why.

Scenario 1

WJ Patch Ltd, a company which owns a small group of jewellery shops, requires a 'working capital line'. This line is to fund the day-to-day requirements of the business and, most importantly, its highly seasonal cash flows. Jewellery shops typically makes two thirds of their sales in one third of the year, i.e. the three months before Christmas (September to December) and the following month in the New Year (January) sales.

Type of bank borrowing most suitable:

....

....

Reason why this bank borrowing is most suitable:

....

....

Scenario 2

St. Mirren Tools Ltd, an engineering company, seeks to finance an extensive factory refurbishment purchasing new machinery with an expected useful line of ten years. This company's business is not subject to any seasonal variations.

Type of bank borrowing most suitable:

....

....

Reason why this bank borrowing is most suitable:

....

....

Task 6

Bank references are commonly used to assess a customer's creditworthiness. When writing references, identify **TWO** parties to whom the bank owes a duty of care. Briefly explain the reasons for this duty.

....

....

....

....

....

Task 7

Spanvall Ltd grants terms of 60 days net to customers, but offers a discount for early settlement of 2% for prompt payment within 14 days. What is the cost of this discount to Spanvall?

....

....

....

....

....

CASH MANAGEMENT AND CREDIT CONTROL (PREVIOUSLY UNIT 9 AND UNIT 14)

QUESTIONS

DECEMBER 1996

This central assessment is in **THREE** sections—all of which are based on **Wilson Ltd**. You are reminded that competence must be achieved in each section. You should therefore aim to complete **EVERY** task in **EACH** section. Write your answers in the spaces provided.

You are advised to spend approximately 1 hour on Section 1, 33 minutes on Section 2 and 87 minutes on Section 3.

SECTION 1

Data

Wilson Limited produces bicycle saddles. By increasing exports, it plans to increase production and sales during the first half of next year. The actual figures for November and December were:

Month (1996)	Production (units)	Sales (units)
November	7,000	7,000
December	8,000	8,000

The plans for the next six months are shown below:

Month (1997)	Production (units)	Sales (units)
January	10,000	8,000
February	12,000	10,000
March	12,000	12,000
April	14,000	13,000
May	15,000	14,000
June	15,000	16,000

- The selling price is £20.50 per unit, with an anticipated price increase to £21.50 per unit from 1 June.
- Raw material costs £4 per unit.
- Wages and other variable costs are £8 per unit.
- Other fixed costs are £1,800 per month rising to £2,200 from 1 May onwards.
- Twenty per cent of sales are for cash, the remainder being paid in full 60 days following delivery.
- Material purchases are paid one month after delivery and are held in stock for one month before entering production.
- Wages and variable and fixed costs are paid in the month of production.
- A new machine costing £450,000 is to be purchased in February to cope with the planned expansion of demand. 20% of payment is to be made on 1 February and the remainder retained until the machine is operational (expected 1 July 1997).
- An advertising campaign is also to be launched, involving payments of £20,000 in each of February and May.
- Corporation tax of £56,000 is due on 30 June 1997.
- The company is financed by share capital of £1 million, a debenture of £0.5 million paying semi-annual interest of 3.5% on 30 June and 31 December.
- The directors plan to pay a dividend of £0.1 per share in May.
- An overdraft of £0.5 million has been agreed with Wilson Ltd's bankers.
- The current overdraft interest rate is 7.2% per annum on the prior month closing balance.
- Interest is received on cash balances at 6.0% per annum on the prior month closing balance.
- On 1 January the firm expects to have £185,000 in the bank.

Task 1.1

Complete the cash budget provided below.

| WILSON LIMITED—Cash Budget 1997 | | | | | | |
| | Jan | Feb | Mar | Apr | May | Jun |
			Month ending (£)			
Inflow						
Receipts from cash sales						
Receipts from debtors						
Interest received						
Total inflows						
Outflows						
Payments to creditors						
Variable costs						
Fixed costs						
Advertising						
Capital expenditure						
Corporation tax						
Dividend						
Interest on overdraft						
Interest on long-term loan						
Total outflows						
Net cash flow						
Opening cash balance						
Closing cash balance						

Task 1.2

An alternative technique to the receipts and payments method used in Task 1.1 for forecasting future cash flows involves preparing a comparison of the present and forecast balance sheets (a 'funds flow' method). **Suggest TWO advantages for EACH technique, and explain briefly how they may be used together.**

(a)   **Suggest TWO advantages for the receipts and payments method.**

....

....

....

....

....

(b)   **Suggest TWO advantages for the FUNDS FLOW technique.**

....

....

....

....

....

....

....

....

....

....

(c)   **Describe how each would be used together.**

....

....

....

....

....

SECTION 2

Task 2.1

Wilson Ltd's long-term cash flow forecast to year ended 1999 suggests a cash surplus of £1 million will be generated in 1998 and £1.75 million in 1999.

The company is considering its future cash management strategy and is considering four business strategies. For EACH of the following four scenarios, suggest what ACTION you would take to manage the cash surplus and the REASON for your recommendation.

(a)   **No further growth in Wilson Ltd's existing business and no plans for further capital investment.**

....

....

....

....

....

....

(b)   **Plans for an acquisition of a cycle parts manufacturer (valued up to £5 million) when a suitable opportunity arises.**

....

....

....

....

....

....

....

(c)   **Development in 1998 and 1999 of several new product lines requiring capital investment of £2.5 million.**

....

....

....

....

....

....

(d) **Phased development of two new product lines requiring capital investment of £1.25 million and the intention to acquire another cycle parts manufacturer (value up to £3 million) when a suitable opportunity arises.**

....

....

....

....

....

....

....

Task 2.2

What are the main factors to consider when investing a cash surplus? Identify THREE factors and briefly explain their importance.

....

....

....

....

....

....

....

....

....

SECTION 3

Task 3.1

You are working in Wilson Ltd's credit control section. The Sales Manager has asked for your views on the credit status of four organisations to whom Wilson Ltd supplies goods. **Using the extracts from the aged analysis of debtors given below, analyse these four accounts and write a memorandum to the Sales Manager using the form on the following page.**

Your memorandum should:

- **provide an opinion of the creditworthiness of the customer and the status of the account**
- **suggest how the account should be managed in the future.**

EXTRACT FROM: AGED ANALYSIS OF DEBTORS

Customer name and address	Current Month £	Total Due £	Up to 30 days £	Up to 60 days £	Up to 90 days £	Over 90 days £
Megacorp PLC Oakham, Rutland	10,000	72,540	11,250	12,250	15,500	23,540
Credit limit	£85,000		Terms of sale: 60 days net			
Goodfellows Cycles Ltd Manchester	9,500	24,000	9,500			5,000
Credit limit	£50,000		Terms of sale: 60 days net			
Hooper-bikes Ltd Sheffield	5,000	26,750	6,250	4,875	5,275	5,350
Credit limit	£25,000		Terms of sale: 60 days net			
Dynamo Cycles Ltd Nottingham	4,500	7,250	2,750			
Credit limit	£7,500		Terms of sale: 30 days net			

MEMORANDUM

Task 3.2

To improve Wilson Ltd's credit control procedures, you have been asked by the Credit Manager, in your position as Credit Analyst, to design a standard form to be sent to a potential customer's trade referees.

Draft a suitable form below.

<h3 style="text-align:center">WILSON LTD TRADE REFERENCE FORM</h3>

CASH MANAGEMENT AND CREDIT CONTROL (PREVIOUSLY UNIT 9 AND UNIT 14)

QUESTIONS

JUNE 1997

This central assessment is in **THREE** sections. You are reminded that competence must be achieved in each section. You should therefore aim to complete **EVERY** task in **EACH** section. Write your answers in the spaces provided.

You are advised to spend approximately 1 hour on Section 1, 1 hour on Section 2 and 1 hour on Section 3.

Any essential calculations should be included within your answer where appropriate.

SECTION 1

Data

EKAT is a charity which provides training and support for people experiencing a wide range of disabilities. EKAT aims to make its employees as economically productive and independent as possible by providing work-based training in one of its agricultural or horticultural projects. It operates a range of activities and is considering a new project, called 'Project Roundabout.'

As a charity, EKAT has a different approach from commercial, private - sector organisations:

- it aims to make a minimum level of profit and create sustainable growth;

- it is important for EKAT to generate enough profit and stable cash flow to ensure its long-term financial viability;

- the financial collapse of the company or any of its projects would be extremely damaging to its employees, who are already struggling to believe they can cope with and succeed in a work environment;

- EKAT must be financially cautious, to prevent the business from becoming insolvent, whilst generating growth and new projects that enable it to take on more employees whom it can help to secure eventual long-term employment in a commercial environment.

Project Roundabout will produce flowering plants to be sold to East Kilbride District Council for use by its Highways Division on roadsides and roundabouts.

As an accounting technician employed by EKAT you have been provided with the following financial details of the project:

Staff costs

Description	Cost per employee	Number required
Project leader	£20,000 p.a.	1
Trainees' wages	£8,000 p.a.	16
Driver	£11,000 p.a.	1

Equipment costs

Description	Cost per unit	Number required
Portakabin	£7,000	1
Protective clothing	£25	32
Rotavators	£1,650	2
Minibus	£10,000	1
Other tools	£1,000	1
Irrigation unit	£5,000	1

- All equipment costs will be incurred at the start of Project Roundabout
- Assume payroll and other operating costs are incurred at the end of each year.
- Assume sales are made at the end of each year.
- 32 sets of clothing will be required to be purchased at the beginning of each year.
- Maintenance costs are semi-variable and are forecast at £1,000 per annum (p.a.) plus 1% of sales.
- Plants are sold in trays of 20 plants.
- A third rotavator will be purchased when production reaches 25,000 trays p.a.

Other operating costs:

Utility costs:

Water rates	£1,200 p.a.
Gas costs	£750 p.a.
Electricity costs	£450 p.a.
Telephone costs	£600 p.a.

Other costs:

Land rent	£1,850 p.a.
Fertiliser	£0.10 per tray of plants produced
Running costs for minibus	£2,500 p.a.

Production estimates:

Year	Tray (of 20 plants)
1	15,000
2	25,000
3	35,000
4 and thereafter	45,000

Each plant is sold for £0.25

Inflation estimates:

Land rent is expected to rise at 4% p.a. The increase in the Retail Price Index (RPI) is expected to remain steady at 5% p.a. Costs can be expected to inflate, from the start of the project, at the following rates:

Income, equipment, fertiliser, minibus and maintenance costs	RPI p.a.
Wages	RPI plus 1% p.a.
Utility costs	RPI minus 1% p.a.

Task 1.1

Prepare a cash flow forecast for Project Roundabout for the first four years of the project using the form provided on the following page.

EKAT — PROJECT ROUNDABOUT
Cash Flow Forecast

End of year	Start of project (0)	1	2	3	4	Total
Sales						
Production (trays)						
Sales (£)						
Payroll costs						
Other operating costs						
Equipment costs						
Opening cash flow						
Total cash flow						
Closing cash flow						

Task 1.2

Identify the options that exist in raising finance for not-for-profit or charitable organisations. Suggest the most appropriate means for EKAT to fund the project.

....

....

....

....

....

....

....

....

....

....

SECTION 2

Task 2.1

An extract from EKAT's aged debtor analysis as at 30 April 1997 is shown on the next page. You should assume the date is 3rd June. Use the following information on transactions which took place during May to update the aged debtor analysis, which follows that for April.

Customer	Information
Gartcosh	Paid invoice K449 £9,000. Invoice K496 remains unpaid. Invoice K521 £5,000 issued.
Strathaven	Paid invoice K495 £7,000. Invoice K511 £6,600 issued.
Coatbridge	Paid invoice K323 £3,000 Invoice K411 remains unpaid. Invoice K502 £4,000 issued.
New Mains	Invoices K289 £8,000 and K487 £2,000 remain unpaid. Invoice K508 £2,775 issued.
Castlemilk	Paid invoice K442 £4,000 Invoice K472 £11,000 remains unpaid.
Rutherglen	Invoice K481 £1,000 remains unpaid.
Cambuslang	Invoice K204 £1,500 remains unpaid.
Easterhouse	Paid invoice K331 £10,000. Invoice K392 £13,000 remains unpaid. Invoice K510 £3,000 issued.
Airdrie	Paid half invoice K234, balance remains unpaid.
Stewartfield	Paid invoice K382 £3,000. Invoice K513 £5,000 issued.

EKAT Aged Debtor Analysis – 30th April 1997 – Credit terms: 30 days

Action
1 Statement
2 1st reminder
3 2nd reminder
4 Telephone call
5 Warning letter
Recovery action implemented

Customer name and ref	Total amount	Invoices not yet due	Outstanding 1 month	Outstanding 2 months	Outstanding 3 months	Outstanding 3+ months	1	2	3	4	5	6
Gartcosh	$14,000		£5,000K496	£9,000K449			03-Apr K496 / 03-MarK449	03-AprK449				
Strathaven	£7,000		£7,000K496				03-AprK495					
Coatbridge	£6,000			£3,000K411	£3,000K323		03-FebK323 / 03-MarK 441	03-MarK323 / 03-AprK441	03-AprK323			
New Mains	£10,000		£2,000K487			£8,000K289	03-JanK487 / 03-AprK487	03-FebK289	03-MarK289	03-AprK289		
Castlemilk	£15,000		£11,000K472	£4,000K442			03-MarK442 / 03-AprK472	03-AprK442				
Rutherglen	£1,000		£1000K481				03-AprK481					
Cambuslang	£1,500					£1,500K204	03-DecK204	03-JanK204	03-FebK204	03-MarK204	03-AprK204	
Easterhouse	£23,000		£13,000k392	£10,000K331			03-FebK331 / 03-AprK392	03-MarK331				
Airdrie	£5,500				£5,500K234		03-FebK234	03-MarK234	03-AprK234			
Stewartfield	£3,000			£3,000K382			03-MarK382	03-AprK382				
TOTALS	£86,000		£39,000	£29,000	£8,500	£9,500						

EKAT Aged Debtor Analysis – 31st May 1997 – Credit terms: 30 days

Customer name and ref	Total amount	Invoices not yet due	Outstanding 1 month	Outstanding 2 months	Outstanding 3 months	Outstanding 3+ months	Action 1	2	3	4	5	6
Gartcosh	$14,000		£5,000K496	£9,000K449			03-Apr K496 03-MarK449	03-AprK449				
Strathaven	£7,000		£7,000K496				03-AprK495					
Coatbridge	£6,000			£3,000K411	£3,000K323		03-FebK323 03-MarK 441	03-MarK323 03-AprK441	03-AprK323			
New Mains	£10,000		£2,000K487			£8,000K289	03-JanK487 03-AprK487	03-FebK289	03-MarK289	03-AprK289		
Castlemilk	£15,000		£11,000K472	£4,000K442			03-MarK442 03-AprK472	03-AprK442				
Rutherglen	£1,000		£1000K481				03-AprK481					
Cambuslang	£1,500					£1,500K204	03-DecK204	03-JanK204	03-FebK204	03-MarK204	03-AprK204	
Easterhouse	£23,000		£13,000K392	£10,000K331			03-FebK331 03-AprK392	03-MarK331				
Airdrie	£5,500				£5,500K234		03-FebK234	03-MarK234	03-AprK234			
Stewartfield	£3,000			£3,000K382			03-MarK382	03-AprK382				
TOTALS	**£86,000**		**£39,000**	**£29,000**	**£8,500**	**£9,500**						

Action
1 Statement
2 1st reminder
3 2nd reminder
4 Telephone call
5 Warning letter
6 Recovery action implemented

Task 2.2

For each customer, outline briefly how that account should be managed.

Gartcosh — a medium-sized, regular customer

....

....

....

....

Coatbridge — a large, major customer

....

....

....

....

New Mains — a medium sized, regular customer

....

....

....

....

Cambuslang — a small and irregular customer

....

....

....

....

Airdrie — a large and irregular customer

....

....

....

....

SECTION 3

Task 3.1

EKAT grants credit terms of 60 days net to its major customers, but offers an early settlement discount of 2.5% for payment within seven days.

What is the cost of this discount?

....

....

....

....

Task 3.2

Why might EKAT choose to offer its major customers such a generous discount? Identify TWO reasons.

....

....

....

....

Task 3.3

Some of EKAT's customers make occasional late payments. After telephoning the customer, it is company policy to write a reminder letter to the customer concerned.

Write a reminder letter to the customer on the headed notepaper provided on the following page, using the details below:

Customer name and address:	Canadian Steel Corporation (UK) Limited, Summerhill Street, Coatbridge, Lanarkshire, ML12 6TY
Account number:	33587
Invoice number:	J548
Contact name:	Margaret Darroch (Director of Finance)
Amount outstanding	£1,634.93
Previous account action:	Four written reminders and three telephone calls. On each occasion payment promised.

EKAT

EKAT,
29, Glen Arroch,
East Mains,
East Kilbride,
G74 7CO

....

....

....

....

....

....

....

....

....

....

....

....

....

....

....

....

....

....

....

....

EKAT ....

◇ FOULKSlynch

Task 3.4

A small subsidiary of EKAT operates a simple manual sales ledger. This is used because it has less than 50 credit customers and only a limited number of credit transactions. Balances are computed monthly using a desk calculator and the aged debtor analysis is carried out manually. This system however provides little credit control information.

List FOUR extra items of information, relating to transactions with customers, which are required for credit control purposes.

....

....

....

....

....

....

....

Task 3.5

The Bank of England performs a number of functions. Identify FIVE of these functions.

....

....

....

....

....

....

Task 3.6

What is the difference between an overdraft and a bullet repayment loan?

....

....

....

CASH MANAGEMENT AND CREDIT CONTROL (PREVIOUSLY UNIT 9 AND UNIT 14)

QUESTIONS

DECEMBER 1997

This central assessment is in THREE sections. You are reminded that competence must be achieved in each section. You should therefore attempt and aim to complete EVERY task in EACH section. Write your answers in the spaces provided.

You are advised to spend approximately 1 hour on Section 1, 1 hour on Section 2 and 1 hour on Section 3.

SECTION 1

Data

Onedin plc operates two divisions: shipping and tourism. The larger division is the Shipping Division, which is capital-intensive and funded by loans which are secured on its ships. The Shipping Division receives its income from shipping cargo and from trading in the value of its ships, which has been rising recently due to undersupply. This division is currently unprofitable.

The other division is the Tourism Division which generates cash flow by selling holidays and taking deposits in the early part of the year, and paying suppliers later in the year.

- Onedin plc is funded by a £200 million loan, secured on the ships. Interest is payable at 8% per annum on 30 April and 31 October.

- A £40 million overdraft and unsecured loan facilities are currently available on demand and discussed with the bank each November

- A ship is to be sold for £25 million in January 1998 and the payment will be received in February 1998.

- Capital expenditure of £15 million is anticipated in the Tourism Division; payment will be on 9 March 1998.

- The Shipping Division is expected to produce cash losses of £10 million per month from November 1997 to February 1998. In March 1998, it is expected to lose £17 million and in April 1998 and May 1998 these losses will remain steady at £15 million per month. From June 1998, a cost-cutting drive is expected to cut losses to £12 million per month.

- The Tourism Division is expected to produce cash flow of £10 million in December 1997 and January 1998, £14 million from February 1998 to April 1998 and £20 million from May to June 1998.

- The overdrafts and unsecured loans incur interest at 7% per annum, payable monthly on the previous month's balance

- Cash surpluses earn interest at a rate of 6% per annum, payable monthly on the previous month's balance.

- A Corporation Tax payment of £6 million is due in March 1998

- A dividend payment of £11 million is anticipated in April 1998

- The opening cash position is £27 million overdrawn

Task 1.1

Using the proforma which follows, calculate Onedin plc's cash budget to 30 June 1998. In your calculations, you should assume interest is payable on an equal month's basis.

ONEDIN PLC
Cash Budget for the six months to June 1998

	£000 Jan	£000 Feb	£000 Mar	£000 April	£000 May	£000 June	£000 Total
Opening position							
Tourism							
Shipping							
Ship trading							
Capital Expenditure							
Taxation							
Dividends							
Interest on loans							
Interest on overdraft							
Interest on cash surplus							
Closing position							

Task 1.2

Onedin plc wants to improve its cash flow position over the next six months. **Identify FIVE steps the company might take, assuming it has no wish to delay payments to suppliers or tighten its collection policy.**

....

....

....

....

....

....

....

1.3 Task

Identify TWO of the most significant risks that affect Onedin plc's cash flow position over the six months to 30 June 1998.

....

....

....

....

....

Task 1.4

Onedin plc has £200 million of loans secured on its ships. **Give THREE reasons why the ships are suitable as security for lending, regardless of their increasing value.**

....

....

....

....

....

SECTION 2

Data

Onedin plc has been approached by Castle Ltd, a producer of road building materials, to transport materials world–wide. Castle Ltd is a privately owned, family business. The company has asked for credit of £25,000 on 60 days terms.

Task 2.1

Study the correspondence (two letters and two trade references) set out after the blank memorandum which follows this page, and consider Castle Ltd's request. Prepare a memo, using the form which follows this page, for the Credit Controller's attention, to recommend how Onedin plc should proceed.

Note: **An additional sheet of memorandum paper is provided if necessary. It is not anticipated that this sheet will need to be used by all candidates.**

MEMO

Note: This page will not need to be used by all candidates.

National Bank plc

Morishall Branch,
25, Levens Street,
London
SE1 4RT

19 November 1997

Credit Controller,
Onedin plc,
1, Morishall Road
London
SE1 9XX

Dear Sir or Madam,

Bank Reference - Castle Ltd

I refer to your letter dated 10 November 1997 in inquiring about the credit worthiness of Castle Ltd. Castle Ltd have been a customer of the Bank for eighteen months. In our view, Castle Ltd is a reasonably constituted company, whose financial resources would appear to be fully employed.

Yours faithfully,

Stephen MacDonald,
Manager

Standard letter to trade referees:

ONEDIN PLC
1, Morishall Road,
London,
SE1 9XX

Telephone: 0171 203 3000
Fax: 0171 203 3001
E-Mail: aziz-cc@ onedin.co.uk
Web Page: http:\\www.onedin.co.uk

PRIVATE AND CONFIDENTIAL

10 November 1997

Credit Controller,
Windsor Haulage Limited,
Speirs Wharf,
London,
SE16 7UH

Dear Sir or Madam,

CREDIT REFERENCE

We recently received a request for credit from Castle Ltd, a prospective customer of ours, which has given your company as a trade referee. I would be grateful if you could assist us by completing the enclosed form and returning it in the stamped addressed envelope provided.

Thank you for your help.

Yours faithfully,

Rita Aziz
Credit Controller

STRICTLY PRIVATE AND CONFIDENTIAL

Name of Referee Company: *WINDSOR HAULAGE LIMITED*

1. **How long have Castle Ltd been trading with you?**

   ONE...**years**   *TWO*...**months**

2. **When Castle Ltd opened an account with you did the company supply you with suitable trade and credit references?**

   ~~YES~~ / NO

3. **What are your normal credit terms for Castle Ltd?**

   Amount: £......*15,000*

Terms:	**Cash**	**Weekly**	**Monthly** *30 DAYS NET*	**Other (please detail below):**

   ....

   ....

   ....

   ....

4. **Does Castle Ltd make payments in accordance with your terms?**

   YES / ~~NO / SLOW PAYER~~

5. **Have you ever had to suspend credit facilities to Castle Ltd?**

   ~~YES~~ / NO

   If YES when?

6. **Please supply any other information which you consider relevant.**

Thank you for completing this questionnaire.

STRICTLY PRIVATE AND CONFIDENTIAL

Name of Referee Company: *CASE WESTERN SHIPPING INC.*

1.   **How long have Castle Ltd been trading with your?**

   THREE...**years**   *FIVE*...**months**

2.   **When Castle Ltd opened an account with you did the company supply you with suitable trade and credit references?**

   YES / ~~NO~~

3.   **What are your normal credit terms for Castle Ltd?**

   Amount: *US$ 100,000 (equivalent £65,000)*

   Terms: **Cash**   **Weekly**   **Monthly**   **Other (please detail below):**
                                                                      ✓

   ....

   ....

   ....

   ....

4.   **Does Castle Ltd make payments in accordance with your terms?**

   YES / ~~NO / SLOW PAYER~~

5.   **Have you ever had to suspend credit facilities to Castle Ltd?**

   YES / ~~NO~~

   If YES when?
   3 years ago

6.   **Please supply any other information which you consider relevant.**

   Castle Ltd is our biggest customer in terms of sales. We can recommend the company without hesitation to you.

Thank you for completing this questionnaire.

Task 2.2

What rights does the Data Protection Act 1984 confer on Castle Ltd, when Onedin plc seeks banks and trade references from its bankers and suppliers? Give reasons for your answer.

....

....

....

....

Task 2.3

Occasionally, Onedin plc needs to write off bad debts. Identify THREE important issues it should consider before doing so.

....

....

....

....

....

....

Task 2.4

Onedin plc is considering passing the responsibility of administering its debtors to a factoring agency. Identify FOUR services that such an agency would provide.

....

....

....

....

....

....

....

SECTION 3

Data

Castle Ltd is considering a change of credit policy which will result in increasing the average collection period from two months to three months. The change in credit policy is expected to increase sales revenue each year by 10%.

You are given the following information about the company

Profit margin	15%
Current sales revenue per year	£120 million
Required rate of return on investment	20%

In answering the tasks below you should assume that the expected increase in sales revenue would retsult in increased stock of £1 million and would reduce the level of creditors by £1 million. You should also assume that all customers take the longer credit period of three months.

Task 3.1

(a)   **Calculate the increase in sales revenue in the year following the change in credit policy.**

....

....

....

(b)   **Calculate the increase in profit in the year following the change in credit policy.**

....

....

....

(c)   **Calculate the net increase in working capital in the year following the change in credit policy.**

....

....

....

....

....

....

....

....

....

....

....

(d)   **Calculate the return on the extra investment.**

....

....

....

....

(e)   **Advise Castle Ltd whether or not it should extend the credit period offered to customers, and the reason why.**

....

....

....

....

Task 3.2

Granting credit to customers incurs additional costs. **Give THREE reasons why an organisation justifies this expense.**

....

....

....

....

....

Task 3.3

Distinguish between seasonal differences and cyclical differences in the context of an organisation's cash flow. Give an example of each.

....

....

....

....

....

....

....

....

....

....

....

Task 3.4

(a)   **In a cash management context, what are index numbers?**

....

....

....

....

....

(b)   **Explain how index numbers might be useful in cash forecasting.**

....

....

....

....

....

ANSWERS

1–2   CASH FLOW AND CASH BUDGETS

1   Solution

(a)   (**Tutorial note:** stock is used up by material usage, and by closing stock. This usage is made up partly from opening stock. The balance must be made up from purchases. This situation is shown in the solution following.)

	June £	July £	August £
Material usage	8,000	9,000	10,000
Closing stock	3,500	6,000	4,000
	11,500	15,000	14,000
Less: Opening stock	5,000	3,500	6,000
Purchases	6,500	11,500	8,000

(b)   (**Tutorial note:** the main points to watch out for are sales receipts and overheads. Tackle sales receipts by calculating separate figures for cash sales (10% of total sales, received in the month of sale) and credit sales (90% of **last month's** sales). For overheads, remember that depreciation is not a cash expense and must therefore be stripped out of the overheads cash cost.)

Cash budgets, June - August

	June £	July £	August £
Receipts of cash			
Cash sales	4,500	5,000	6,000
Credit sales	29,500	40,500	45,000
	34,000	45,500	51,000
Cash payments			
Wages	12,000	13,000	14,500
Overheads	6,500	7,000	8,000
Direct materials	6,500	11,500	8,000
Taxation	-	25,000	-
	25,000	56,500	30,500
Surplus/(deficit) for month	9,000	(11,000)	20,500
Opening balance	11,750	20,750	9,750
Closing balance	20,750	9,750	30,250

(c)   Cash budgets are an important part of business planning. They highlight future surpluses of cash (enabling managers to make appropriate plans for investing the surplus) and shortfalls of cash (enabling managers to take appropriate action in advance, perhaps by advising their bank of overdraft requirements or raising funds from other sources).

2   Solution

(a)   Production budget (units)

	January	February	March
Sales	5,000	4,000	6,000
Add: Closing stock (W)	2,000	3,000	4,000
Less: Opening stock	(2,500)	(2,000)	(3,000)
Production	4,500	5,000	7,000

WORKING

Closing stock = 50% of following month's sales.

(b)   Cash budget

	January	February	March
Receipts			
Cash sales from debtors (W1)	130,000	185,000	221,250
Payments (W2)			
To material suppliers	30,000	67,500	75,000
Labour	40,500	45,000	63,000
Overheads	62,100	62,200	67,200
	132,600	174,700	205,200
Net cash inflow/(outflow)	(2,600)	10,300	16,050
Balance brought forward	3,000	400	10,700
Balance carried forward	400	10,700	26,750

WORKINGS

(W1)   Sales receipts

		January £	February £	March £
Debtors b/f	- Nov	22,500		
	- Dec	45,000	22,500	
Current sales	- Jan (£250,000)	62,500	112,500	56,250
	- Feb (£200,000)		50,000	90,000
	- Mar (£300,000)			75,000
		130,000	185,000	221,250

Note: it is assumed that the debtors of the beginning of January are shown gross of bad debts

(W2)

	January	February	March	
Production (units)	4,500	5,000	7,000	
	£	£	£	
Materials usage (@ £15)	67,500	75,000	105,000	(£30,000 b/f
Paid	Feb	March	April	paid Jan)
Labour (@£9)	40,500	45,000	63,000	
Paid	Jan	Feb	March	

◈ FOULKS*lynch*

Total overhead

Fixed (£576,000/12)		48,000	48,000	48,000
Less: Depreciation		(4,800)	(4,800)	(4,800)
		43,200	43,200	43,200
Variable (@£4)		18,000	20,000	28,000
		61,200	63,200	71,200
Paid: 50% current month		30,600	31,600	35,600
50% next month			30,600	31,600
		30,600	62,200	67,200
+ b/f		31,500		
		62,100		

3   Solution

STEP 1

	Sales	Cash received		
		July	August	September
	£	£	£	£
May	600,000	54,000	-	-
June	800,000	240,000	72,000	-
July	360,000	216,000	108,000	32,400
August	420,000	-	252,000	126,000
September	600,000	-	-	360,000
		510,000	432,000	518,400

STEP 2

	£
Obsolete stock at cost	30,000
Normal sales price	
$\frac{100}{60} \times £30,000$	50,000
Realised ½ × £50,000	25,000

STEP 3

		£	£	£
(i)	10 July - Balance b/d			370,000

(ii)	10 August - sales in July		360,000	

Cost of goods sold (60%)   216,000

Less: Opening stock	(840,000)	
Less: Obsolete stock	30,000	

(810,000)

Add: Closing stock 60%
(420,000 + 600,000 + 540,000)   936,000

126,000

342,000

(iii)	10 September - sales in August		420,000	

Cost of goods sold (60%)   252,000

Less: Opening stock	(936,000)

Add: Closing stock 60%
(600,000 + 540,000
+ 480,000)   972,000

36,000

288,000

STEP 4   **The cash budget**

	July	August	September
Receipts:			
Receipts from debtors	510,000	432,000	518,400
Obsolete stock	25,000	-	-
	535,000	432,000	518,400
	£	£	£
Payments:			
Payments to creditors	370,000	342,000	288,000
Expenses	160,620	118,800	158,400
Dividends	-	-	40,000
Advertising	-	10,000	15,000
Capital expenditure	3,000	3,000	3,000
Corporation tax	-	-	60,000
Bank loan	-	-	288,400
	533,620	473,800	852,800
Net cash inflow/(outflow)	1,380	(41,800)	(334,400)
Balance	100,000	101,380	59,580
Balance/ (deficiency) at month end	101,380	59,580	(274,820)

4   Solution

	Jul £'000	Aug £'000	Sep £'000	Oct £'000	Nov £'000	Dec £'000	Total £'000
Receipts:							
Sales	210	200	200	200	200	200	1,210
New issue of share capital	-	-	-	30	-	-	30
Payments:							
Expenses and purchases	160	150	150	150	150	150	910
Expenses and purchases	24	24	24	24	24	24	144
Plant	12	25	13	-	50	-	100
Stock	-	20	-	-	-	-	20
Tax	-	-	-	-	-	30	30
Dividends	-	24	-	-	-	-	24
	196	243	187	174	224	204	1,228
Surplus/(deficiency)	14	(43)	13	56	(24)	(4)	12
Opening balance	40	54	11	24	80	56	40
Closing balance	54	11	24	80	56	52	52

5   Solution

(a)

	Sept £	Oct £	Nov £	Dec £	Jan £	Feb £
RECEIPTS						
Cash sales (W1)	18,240	15,200	17,100	16,720	15,960	19,000
Credit sales (W2)	30,000	28,800	24,000	27,000	26,400	25,200
Capital		8,000				
	48,240	52,000	41,100	43,720	42,360	44,200
PAYMENTS						
Purchases (W3)	18,800	19,600	17,600	17,000	19,800	17,200
Wages (W4)	6,800	6,000	6,500	6,400	6,200	7,000
Fixed costs (W5)	6,000	6,000	6,000	6,000	6,000	6,000
Capital	15,000		10,000			4,000
Corporation tax			44,000			
	46,600	31,600	84,100	29,400	32,000	34,200
Surplus/(Deficit)	1,640	20,400	(43,000)	14,320	10,360	10,000
Balance b/f	5,000	6,640	27,040	(15,960)	(1,640)	8,720
Balance c/f	6,640	27,040	(15,960)	(1,640)	8,720	18,720

(b)   A spreadsheet is a computer modelling package which comprises rows and columns which intersect to form cells in a matrix. It can be seen that this is the layout used in (a) above.

Each cell may be used to store either a label (description); a value; or a formula. The formula may be referenced to the contents of other cells which can automate the calculation of many values in applications such as the cash budget in (a) above.

The spreadsheet may be used simply as an efficient and powerful calculator; however, it is also a powerful presentations device with graphic representations of the data being available. In this regard the user must segregate the output presentation and data entry areas of the spreadsheet.

Using part (a) as an example, the row and column headings would be as shown above. The sales values for each month would then be inserted into an input area together with the percentages for cash/credit sales etc. The equivalent of working 3 would also be included in this area.

Formulae would then be entered in the input area to calculate intermediate values (eg, stock used in W3) and in the output area to link with the input area. Some values (eg, the capital receipt and payments) would be keyed directly into the output area since no further calculations are required. Where the same formula is used for a number of time periods, then it would be entered once and copied to the columns of the other periods.

Any of the input variables may then be changed and the effect on the final output will be automatically calculated, this is known as What-If analysis.

WORKINGS

(W1)   Since 60% of sales are credit sales, 40% are cash sales, eg,

	£
September cash sales = £48,000 × 40% =	19,200
5% discount on £19,200	960
	18,240

(W2)   August credit sales are paid in September, and so on.

Credit sales = 60% so the September receipt = 60% × £50,000 = £30,000

(W3)	July	Aug	Sept	Oct	Nov	Dec
Sales:						
Stock used						
(40% of sales)	17,600	20,000	19,200	16,000	18,000	17,600
Opening stock						
(50% of 40% of sales)	(8,800)	(10,000)	(9,600)	(8,000)	(9,000)	(8,800)
Closing stock						
(50% of 40% of						
next months sales)	10,000	9,600	8,000	9,000	8,800	8,400
Extra stock					2,000	
PURCHASES	18,800	19,600	17,600	17,000	19,800	17,200
Paid in	Sept	Oct	Nov	Dec	Jan	Feb

(W4)   10% of sales + £2,000

eg, September:
(10% × £48,000) + £2,000 = £6,800

(W5)   £7,500 – £1,500 Depreciation : £6,000

3   FORECASTING TECHNIQUES

1   Solution

(a)   To calculate the four quarterly moving average trend, the sum of each set of 4 quarters, moving down the data one quarter at a time, must be calculated. The sum of every two of these values is then calculated to give an eight period total. These totals are then all divided by eight to arrive at the trend figures. This is shown below.

Year	Qtr	Revenue values (000's)	Sum of 4 quarters	Sum of 8 quarters	Trend
1	1	49			
	2	37	211		
	3	58	212	423	52.875 (423 ÷ 8)
	4	67	213	425	53.125 (425 ÷ 8)
2	1	50	214	427	53.375
	2	38	215	429	53.625
	3	59	216	431	53.875
	4	68	218	434	54.250
3	1	51	219	437	54.625
	2	40	221	440	55.000
	3	60	220	441	55.125
	4	70	222	442	55.250
4	1	50	223	445	55.625
	2	42			
	3	61			

(b)   To calculate the seasonal factors another calculation is necessary.

If using the additive model, the components of the time series are shown to be added together ie,

Data (D) = Trend (T) + Seasonal variation (S)

hence the seasonal factors can be calculated by subtracting the trend from the actual data.

Year	Qtr	Actual data	Trend	Actual-trend
1	3	58	52.875	5.125
	4	67	53.125	13.875
2	1	50	53.375	−3.375
	2	38	53.625	−15.625
	3	59	53.875	5.125
	4	68	54.250	13.75
3	1	51	54.625	−3.625
	2	40	55.000	−15
	3	60	55.125	4.875
	4	70	55.250	14.75
4	1	50	55.625	−5.625

The deviations (actual − trend) are now collected together to calculate the seasonal variation. For each quarter, in the form of a table, the total and average for each quarter is calculated.

The total of the averages should equal 0. If this doesn't equal zero, the difference is divided equally between the 4 quarters, and added to each average figure to give the final seasonal variation value.

Year	Q1	Q2	Q3	Q4
1	-	-	5.125	13.875
2	−3.375	−15.625	5.125	13.75
3	−3.625	−15.00	4.875	14.75
4	−5.625	-	-	-
Total	−12.625	−30.625	15.125	42.375
Number of values	3	2	3	3
Average	−4.208	−15.313	5.042	14.125 = −0.354
Difference adjustment	0.0885	0.0885	0.0885	0.0885
Seasonal variation	−4.1195	−15.2245	4.1305	14.2135
=	−4	−15	5	14

(c)   To forecast the revenue for the next four quarters; this can be done by eye ie,

(i)   Plot a graph of the trend
(ii)   By reading the graph, establish the forecast of the trend for the four quarters.
(iii)   Adjust the forecasted trend by the appropriate seasonal variation.

When using the additive model the seasonal variation must be added to the forecast figure.

2   Solution

(a)

Year	Sales ('000)	Sums in 3's	Moving average trend
1	50		
2	59	155	51.7
3	46	159	53.0
4	54	165	55.0
5	65	170	56.7
6	51	176	58.7
7	60	181	60.3
8	70	186	62.0
9	56	192	64.0
10	66	198	66.0
11	76		

(b)   **Brand Y**

**Annual sales of Brand Y and trend
Years 1-11**

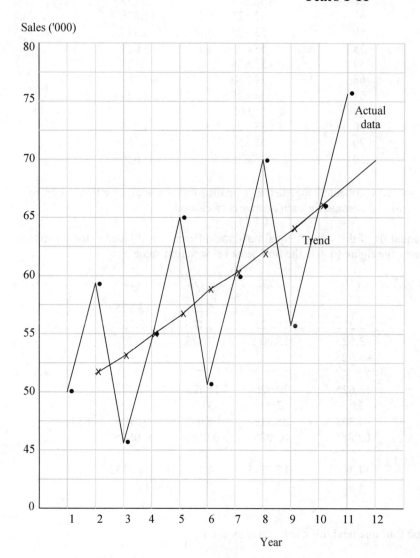

Sales ('000)

(c)   The annual sales data shows a marked cyclical pattern of 3 years.

Year 12 sales would be expected to be less than the trend assuming this pattern continues.

Looking at the sales-trend values for corresponding years in this cycle:

$$\text{Yr 9} \quad 56 - 64 \quad = -8$$

$$\text{Yr 6} \quad 51 - 58.7 \quad = -7.7$$

$$\text{Yr 3} \quad 46 - 53 \quad = -7.$$

$$\text{Mean cyclical movement} \quad = \frac{-8 - 7.7 - 7}{3}$$

$$= \frac{-22.7}{3}$$

$$= -7.6$$

Sales forecast for Year 12 = Trend + cyclical variation.

(Assuming an additive model.)

The trend value for Year 12 can be estimated from the graph by extending the trend line in the direction of the last pair of points. (This is shown by the dotted line on the graph.)

$T = 69.5$

Forecast $=$ $69.5 - 7.6$

$=$ 61.9

The sales forecast for Year 12 is 61,900 units.

The assumptions made are:

(i)   The trend will continue to rise.
(ii)   Brand Y has not reached market saturation point.
(iii)   The cyclical pattern will continue.

4-5   THE ECONOMY AND BANKS

1   Solution

If the business has an overdraft then the business is a debtor of the bank (owes the bank money) and the bank is a creditor of the business (the business owes the bank the amount of the overdraft).

2   Solution

When the cheque for £150 is presented for payment (assuming that there have been no further additions to the funds in Arthur's current account) then the bank will have two options:

- either to refuse to pay on the cheque and return it to the bank where it was paid in marked 'refer to drawer'; or

- to pay the cheque in full causing Arthur's account to go into overdraft.

The bank is not required to pay the cheque in part ie, just the £130 that there is in the current account.

3   Solution

(a)   AM Baker and JS Baker
(b)   National Southern Bank
(c)   L Fuller

4   Solution

(a)   This cheque has an "A/c payee" crossing which means that it must be paid directly into a bank account. However the back of the cheque has been signed by the payee, B Moore, and it would appear that a special endorsement has been made to Peter Fleming. An "A/c payee" cheque, however, cannot be endorsed.

(b)   No errors.

(c)   This cheque has not been signed and is therefore not valid.

(d)   On this cheque the figures show £178.18 but the words are "one hundred and eighty seven pounds and 18 pence". This makes the cheque invalid.

5   Solution

This is a special crossing and it indicates to the bank on which the cheque is drawn (the National Southern Bank) that payment is only to be made into an account at the bank named, in this case Lloyds Bank.

6   Solution

- date (including year);
- payee details (correct name of the supermarket);
- amount is correct;
- words and figures agree;
- cheque is signed;
- signature agrees with that on cheque guarantee card;
- bank details agree with cheque guarantee card;
- sale does not exceed the guarantee amount;
- guarantee card has not expired;
- write cheque guarantee card number, card limit and expiry date on the back of the cheque.

7 Solution

The bank's position is that only one cheque supported by a cheque guarantee card can be used for each transaction.

(a)   Therefore if Phil is to take the goods away immediately the seller runs the risk of one of the cheques not being honoured.

(b)   If the goods are to be delivered in one week's time then this gives the seller long enough for the cheques to be paid into his bank account and work through the clearing system. Once the cheques have cleared the seller will know whether or not the cheques have been honoured and therefore whether valid payment has been received for the goods.

8 Solution

This means that Jones Ltd's bank has refused to pay the cheque. This will usually be because Jones Ltd does not have enough funds in his account at the time. You should therefore contact the drawer, Jones Ltd, and request some other form of payment, a new cheque in the case of Jones' current account having sufficient funds at this later date, or, possibly, return of the goods supplied.

6–8   TREASURY AND RAISING FINANCE

1   Solution

(a)   Financial intermediaries can be divided into those which are banks and those which are non-banks. However, there is increasingly some blurring of the distinction between both types of institution as many have expanded their functions and the services they provide, as a result of the increasing competition in the financial services sector and the globalisation of their markets.

The main bank financial intermediaries are the following:

- Commercial banks, which offer both primary services (ie, those of money transmission) and secondary services (ie, accepting deposits and making loans) as well as a variety of other financial services to both the retail sector (small transactions) and the wholesale sector (large transactions).

- Discount houses, which deal in the secondary bill market - this means that in effect they do wholesale business on a short-term basis.

- The National Savings Bank, which accepts deposits predominantly from the retail sector and lends to the public sector.

- Overseas banks in the UK, which take part in the Euro-currency and Eurobond markets.

- Consortium banks are large conglomerates which lend money in very large amounts to finance major industrial projects.

- The Bank of England, which is the central bank of the UK and as such plays a supervisory and monitoring role in the economy. It does perform some banking functions insofar as it intermediates between the commercial banks and also between the government and the private sector.

The main non-bank financial intermediaries are the following:

- Building societies, which deal predominantly with the retail sector, although their wholesale business is expanding. On the whole they accept deposits from savers and lend to finance house purchase, but they now offer a much wider range of 'banking' services than previously, including primary money transmission facilities.

- Insurance companies and pension funds, which accept money on a very long-term basis from those paying into life assurance and pension schemes, and use the money to make a wide range of investments.

- Unit trusts and investment trusts in which people buy units/shares and which invest in a wide-ranging portfolio of investments.

(b)   Both bank and non bank financial institutions have one thing in common: they bring together the surplus sector of the economy with the deficit sector; they borrow money from those individuals and companies which have more money than they currently need and lend it to those who have less than they currently need. This is the basic principle of financial intermediation. In doing this they eliminate certain problems which would otherwise prevent the funds of the surplus sector from becoming available to the deficit sector.

Such institutions make links between different groups of people who would not otherwise know each other - the lender who deposits money in a bank does not have to look for someone who wants to borrow the money, but lets the bank complete the transaction indirectly. The **information gap** is therefore bridged by the intermediary.

The existence of large institutions also allows **aggregation** to take place. Many borrowers want more money than single small savers can provide, but a bank, or other intermediary, is able to accept a very large number of smaller deposits and aggregate these into larger amounts for loan purposes.

Financial institutions provide **risk transformation**. Many people with surplus funds would be unwilling to lend all their savings to one or two borrowers because of the risk of non-repayment - they would be reluctant to 'put all their eggs into one basket'. A bank, however, provides a relatively risk-free place to deposit savings. As a bank it lends its total deposits to a very large number of borrowers, and because it is a huge company with considerable reserves, it can calculate, and withstand, likely bad debts and ensure that it receives back, with interest, the money it has lent. Insurance companies are another good example of companies which 'pool' risks.

Financial institutions carry out **maturity transformation**. Another obstacle to lending and borrowing without the presence of intermediaries is (in many cases) the desire on the part of the lender to receive the money back sooner than the borrower wishes or is able to repay it. A financial intermediary is able to give liquidity to those depositors who want it and at the same time to allow many borrowers a longer time to repay - a building society is a good example of this, as much of its lending is done on a very long-term basis. The intermediary is thus able to combine short-term liabilities with longer-term assets. It can do this as long as it has an adequate reserve of liquid assets, based on its knowledge of how much money it needs to repay daily, on average, to those depositors who require liquidity. Many depositors are happy to leave their money for long periods of time, and the intermediary uses this money.

If financial intermediaries were not present in the economy individual savers would not know who to lend to, would not be able to supply the required amount nor be willing to accept the risk and the loss of liquidity. The intermediaries thus ensure that lending and borrowing take place on a much larger scale than could be possible without them.

It is of vital economic importance that such lending and borrowing should take place. From the viewpoint of surplus units in the economy, it is important that people with money to lend should be able to find a safe place to put their savings, which will give them the liquidity they need and at the same time pay them a rate of interest. Many individuals and companies rely on the income they receive from interest payments.

On the other hand from the viewpoint of intended deficit units it is vital that people who need to borrow should be able to do so. Economic growth is based on investment; ie, the expansion and modernisation of industry and commerce, and investment comes from borrowed funds. Governments need to borrow to be able to finance important areas of public expenditure; companies need to borrow to finance expansion, purchases of new equipment etc and also to finance short-term trading imbalances; and individuals need to borrow to be able to buy houses and to enable them to consume much of the output of industry which would otherwise remain unsold. Borrowing leads to employment and growth.

2   Solution

All firms finance all their activities by borrowing, as can be seen from a balance sheet where every pound sterling of asset is represented by a pound sterling of liabilities. Public limited companies have more and wider opportunities to obtain finance than do other, smaller firms. Their liabilities can be divided into two main categories; equity and debt.

Equity is money lent to the company by the owners (ie, the shareholders) and it takes the form of share capital and reserves, the latter of which are held on behalf of the shareholders. Debt is lent to the company by non-owners (ie, creditors), who may buy debentures (loan stock) or who may, like banks, make loans. The relationship between the amount of equity and the amount of debt on a company's balance sheet is important and it is called its 'gearing ratio'. A company which has a higher proportion of equity and a lower proportion of debt is said to be low-geared, and this is preferable to the opposite. This is because creditors are expected, by law, to suffer less risk than shareholders. A company must expect to have to repay its loans in full, with interest, even if it has to make a loss in so doing, whereas shareholders' capital is not returnable (to get his money back, a shareholder must sell his shares to someone else). In addition, the company has no agreed rate of dividend which it must pay to its owners; ordinary shareholders receive dividends according to the amount of profit earned by the company.

Ordinary shares are the most important part of a company's equity. They are issued up to a maximum authorised amount when the company is first formed and their owners have voting rights (control over the company to the extent of their shareholdings). These shares carry no fixed dividend; the annual dividend is decided each year according to the company's profit. A company which wants to raise more capital can issue new shares to the general public, and will often arrange for the issue to be underwritten by a merchant bank. Alternatively it could make a rights issue to existing shareholders, in proportion to their shareholdings; this means that they would have the right to buy these shares, usually at a discount, before the shares are offered elsewhere. The ability of a company to raise finance through share issues will depend upon the current (and therefore expected) performance of that company on its profits forecasts. A successful company, whose existing shares have a high market value, should therefore have no problem in raising new equity capital.

Equity also includes shareholders' reserves, some of which may be able to be utilised to finance the purchase of additional assets. Retained or 'ploughed-back' profits are in fact an important source of finance and one which can be easily drawn from. However, there is a cost, which is the opportunity cost of the rate of interest the company could have earned from lending the money elsewhere.

Preference shares can also be issued. These are not strictly equity capital as their holders have limited voting rights and are restricted to a standard rate of annual dividend so that, although they take precedence over ordinary shares in the distribution of profit, they do not fully participate in profit. They are, however, a source of finance, although the amount of money which companies raise in this way is, in practice, limited.

The money raised by a company from equity goes for the most part to finance the purchase of fixed assets. This could involve expansion of the firm, for instance an extension to a factory or a shop opening a new branch; the purchase of new, more advanced machinery and equipment; the replacement or maintenance of existing equipment.

Debt is lent by creditors. These can be people who have purchased debentures (loan stock), which pay a fixed rate of annual interest that is classed as a normal expense by the company. Some debentures are redeemable after a period of years. A company can also raise funds by borrowing from a financial institution like a bank or merchant bank. Such loans can be for varying lengths of time, from short to medium to long term. Long- and medium-term agreements would normally be to finance expansion and the purchase of fixed assets, whereas short-term loans might be to finance the cash flow problems which arise from trade. The rate of interest which a company will be charged on a loan will depend, not only on the general level of rates, but within that level, on the status of the company. The more profitable and creditworthy it is, the less risk exists of non-repayment and the lower the interest rate the bank will charge. The rate will also depend on the length of time over which the loan will be repaid (other things being equal, the longer the term the higher the interest rate) and on the amount borrowed (the larger the amount, the lower the rate). Large reputable companies who need to borrow considerable amounts can therefore negotiate more favourable terms.

The government may also make finance available to a company, either as a grant or as a loan with favourable terms. Government help to industry is more easily available when firms move to the less developed areas of the country (ie, those areas where unemployment is higher), and this forms a part of government regional policy.

Short-term finance is also important to a company, as it allows it to accommodate cash flow problems. A firm would prefer not to have to pay for its supplies of raw materials, components etc until it has been able to sell the finished product and receive the money. Short-term credit allows it to bridge the gap. This kind of financing is important because however profitable a company may be on paper, it can be declared insolvent if it cannot meet its short-term commitments. Such finance can come from a bank overdraft (some companies work on a permanent overdraft basis up to an agreed amount); from accepting bills of exchange (which are more than likely to be discounted at a bank); or from receiving an extended payment period from trade creditors themselves. This cost must be balanced against the credit period which the company is expected to allow to its debtors.

Finally there is leasing, which is an alternative to borrowing offered by banks and finance houses. Instead of receiving a loan and buying new equipment, the company leases the equipment from the bank in return for a 'rental' charge.

3   Solution

The Stock Market is a financial intermediary which brings together individuals with different financial requirements. One of its functions is to enable those who need funds to be matched with those who have a surplus of funds. One example of this might be when a private company goes public, the owner realising some of his assets by selling off part or all of his interest in the company. Alternatively, companies needing money to carry out investment projects can raise the funds by issuing securities in the primary market.

The secondary market is the other most important role carried out by the Stock Exchange. This refers to the purchase and sale of second-hand shares and bonds, those which are already held by investors, rather than newly-issued securities.

Long-term capital can be defined in a number of ways, but the usual period over which long-term funds are lent is ten years or more. There are very many types of long-term capital which a company may issue, but essentially it has a choice of three basic categories: ordinary shares, preference shares or loan stock.

Ordinary shares, or equity, are held by the owners of the company. Each share represents a share in the assets of the company and entitles its owner to a dividend, paid out of the profits of the company. The dividend is variable both upwards and downwards, although in practice, dividends per share tend to rise slowly over time. In general, ordinary shares also confer the right to vote on their owner.

Preference shares do not represent ownership of the company, nor do they carry votes. They are entitled to a fixed dividend, which must be paid before the ordinary shareholders receive a dividend. If profits are not high enough to pay the dividend, it remains unpaid, although if the shares are cumulative, all unpaid dividends must be paid as soon as the company makes sufficient profits. Preference shares are more akin to loan stock than they are to equity.

Loan stock has many different names, the most familiar ones being debentures or bonds. This is debt capital, normally carrying fixed rate interest. The loan is usually made for a specific number of years, after which it is repaid (although a company may issue irredeemable loan stock, which is never repaid). This is different from ordinary and preference shares, which are usually not redeemed by the company; investors wishing to realise their investment sell their shares on to other investors.

The main advantage of raising long-term funds on the Stock Market is the fact that it provides a regulated and ordered way of finding individuals or organisations with money they want to lend. In addition to this function, the secondary market gives assurance to investors that they will be able to realise their investments when they need to. As large volumes of securities are traded on the Stock Market every day, people are relatively safe in tying up their money for apparently long periods of time. Should they need funds, they can liquidate their investments by selling the securities on to somebody else. This means that companies do not have to find investors who are willing to lend money indefinitely or for many years at a time.

Raising equity or debt both have advantages and disadvantages. Equity is useful as the dividends paid depend on profits, so can be reduced or cancelled in times of difficulty. On the other hand, bringing in new shareholders dilutes the control of the company and subjects the original owners to controls and regulations which they may find onerous.

Debt receives a fixed interest payment which is tax deductible, unlike dividends. This makes debt a fairly cheap form of finance, as the payment of interest is offset to a certain extent by the saving of tax. However, debt agreements usually carry with them the right of the debt holders to force the company into liquidation if interest payments are not met.

One of the main criticisms levelled at the Stock Market and those who provide funds through it, is the short-termism. Share ownership, although perhaps wider than it once was, is concentrated in the hands of a few large institutions, such as pension funds, insurance companies and investment and unit trusts. These institutions are often accused of being interested only in short-term gains, concentrating on dividend payouts and fast capital growth. This means that companies are forced into making short-term decisions to satisfy the institutions, rather than considering the longer term and, for example, carrying out research and development, which may use up cash in the present, but will increase future profits. This problem is one of the reasons behind the spate of public companies going private in the mid 1990s, such as Richard Branson's Virgin Group.

Another area of complaint which was noted many years ago, but which is less of a problem today, is the lack of funds available for risky or small ventures. The big institutions are reluctant to make such investments, and the cost of raising money on the Stock Exchange makes it prohibitive for all but the largest companies. Other sources of capital, in particular venture capital companies, have stepped in to fill this need.

Finally, a company always risks not having its shares fully subscribed by the public, although issues are usually underwritten to ensure that shares can be placed with some investor. The most notorious underwriting problem was encountered by the Government, when it sold off shares in British Petroleum around the time of the Stock Market crash in October 1977. The issue was under-subscribed, forcing the Government to turn to the underwriters, who were extremely reluctant to fulfil their role of buying the outstanding shares.

4   Solution

Task 1

Cheques sent to wrong person in the organisation.

Cheques held by an individual before they are banked.

Cheques NOT paid into the bank daily.

Task 2

Bank Name

Bank Address

Sort Code

Account Name

Account Number

Task 3

Discover if the paying company has difficulties making payment on due date.

Find out if the means of payment creates difficulties to the payer.

Task 4

To establish the overall cash/borrowing portion and know the amount of cash available at any given point in time.

5   Solution

Task 1

Short-term, highly liquid investments which are readily convertible to cash.

Task 2

Bills of exchange
Certificates of deposit
Government securities
Local authority short-term loans.

Task 3

On demand.

6   Solution

(a)   **Better control of financial risk**

By determining and maintaining the proper level of cash within a company in accordance with the organisation's financial procedures and within defined authorization limits.

(b)   **Opportunity for profit**

By reducing to a minimum the opportunity cost associated with maintaining cash balances in excess of company's operating needs. Earnings (or surpluses) are improved by freeing up surplus cash for investment purposes while reducing interest charged through minimising borrowing.

(c)   **Strengthened balance sheet**

By reducing or eliminating cash balances in excess of target balances and putting surplus cash to work by investing (eg, in the overnight money market);by reducing or eliminating cash borrowing and keeping interest costs as low as possible.'

(d)   **Increased confidence with customers, suppliers, banks and shareholders**

By having access to funds to disburse to suppliers (creditors), banks (interest, fees and principal payments) and shareholders (dividends) when due. By providing good instructions to customers (debtors) to enable the organisation to convert receipts into usable bank deposits.

7   Solution

Factoring operates on a continual basis whereas invoice discounting operates usually on a piecemeal basis.

Factoring covers all debts, invoice discounting covers a particular selection of invoices.

The factoring company is responsible for the Sales Ledger and debt collection – with invoice discounting, the supplier is responsible for the accounting and debt collection.

8   Solution

Any TWO from:

- flexible means of finance
- short term loan finance
- repayable on demand
- attractive pricing (usually just over market rates)

9 BASIC LAW OF CONTRACT

1 Solution

(a) Consideration must exist means that every simple contract must be supported by consideration. In contrast to a simple contract, consideration is not required to support an agreement made by deed.

Consideration may be defined as the act or forbearance, promised or actual - **Dunlop v Selfridge** - which each party gives.

Consideration must have value means that what is offered as consideration must have **some** economic or monetary value however small. Thus in **Thomas v Thomas** the promise of rent of £1 was valuable consideration. By way of contrast, in **White v Bluett** a promise to cease complaining was not consideration because such a promise had no value.

Consideration need not be adequate means that the respective promises of each party are not required to equate in value. Thus in **Chappell v Nestle** a record was offered for sale in exchange for three chocolate bar wrappers and 1s 6d. It was held that the wrappers were valuable consideration as they were worth something: the fact that their value together with the money did not equate in value with the value of the record was not material.

(b) As stated above each party's act or forbearance may be in the form of a promise or it may be actual.

Consideration in the form of a promise, also called executory consideration, is an undertaking to do something in the future. For example, if today X and Y exchange promises that next week X will deliver a car to Y and Y will then pay £50, their promises today to do something next week constitute consideration with the effect that a binding contract exists from today.

Consideration which is actual, also called executed consideration, arises where a promise is made in return for the performance of an act. Until the act is done by the promisee he has not provided consideration and therefore the other is not bound by his promise until then. In **Carlill v Carbolic Smoke Ball**, for example, the respondent promised a reward of £100 to any person who, having used their smoke ball in the prescribed manner, caught influenza. Mrs Carlill made no reciprocal promise so she was not bound to use the smoke ball but as soon as she did use it she had provided consideration for the respondent's promise and both became bound.

Past consideration is that which has been wholly performed before the other party makes his promise. As a general rule past consideration is insufficient to constitute consideration. In **Re McArdle**, for example, M carried out some repairs to a house for which C afterwards promised payment. It was held that C was not bound by his promise since M's acts were past consideration.

However, there are exceptions to the rule that consideration must not be past. First, the Bills of Exchange Act 1882 states that an antecedent obligation is sufficient to constitute value for a cheque or other bill of exchange. Second, the Limitation Act 1980 states that past consideration is sufficient to support a written acknowledgement of a debt in order to re-start time running for the purpose of calculating the limitation period within which any action for the debt must be brought.

Note: 1 Cases which could have been cited as alternatives to **Re McArdle** are **Eastwood v Kenyon** and **Roscorla v Thomas**.

2 You should take care to distinguish these cases on past consideration from such cases as **Re Casey's Patents** and **Lampleigh v Braithwait** where a service was requested, then carried out, and then a promise to pay was made. In both cases the circumstances showed that the request carried an implied promise to pay: the later actual promise then being treated as the mere fixing of the amount; and accordingly the performance of the service was not past when compared to the implied promise.

(c) As a general rule a promise to perform an existing duty is insufficient to amount to consideration. This is so whether the existing duty is imposed by law or whether it is imposed by contract.

An example of the former occurred in **Collins v Godefroy** where the defendant promised to pay a sum of money to the plaintiff if the plaintiff attended court and gave evidence. The plaintiff attended as agreed but the defendant refused to pay. The plaintiff sued the defendant on his promise. It was held that the plaintiff must fail since as he was already under a legal duty to attend court his attendance was insufficient to constitute consideration for the defendant's promise.

An example of the latter arose in **Stilk v Myrick** where some sailors were promised extra money if they continued to serve on a voyage. Since they were already under a contractual duty to serve on the voyage, their service was insufficient to constitute consideration for the promise of extra money. The recent case of **Williams v Roffey** distinguished **Stilk v Myrick**. In the **Williams** case R contracted to refurbish a block of flats within a certain time period. The contract provided for payment of liquidated damages for time delays. R sub-contracted the carpentry to W for the sum of £20,000. Part way through it was realised that W had underpriced the sub-contract and R promised to pay £10,300 extra money to W to ensure he continued with the carpentry and complete it on time. When R then refused to pay the extra £10,300 W sued. It was held that W had provided sufficient consideration because although he had merely done that which he was contractually obliged to do, it nevertheless conferred a benefit on R in that he thereby avoided time penalties and the cost and aggravation of employing other carpenters to do the work. This decision is very difficult to reconcile with **Stilk v Myrick**.

If a party does more than his existing legal (or contractual) duty - **Glasbrook Bros v Glamorgan** and **Hartley v Ponsonby**, the extra constitutes sufficient consideration. In **Glasbrook Bros v Glamorgan** the appellants promised to pay a sum of money to the local authority if the police would provide protection for their mine in the form of a stationary force. It was held that the local authority had gone beyond their existing legal duty (which was to provide a mobile force) and had thus provided sufficient consideration for the appellants' promise of money.

Exceptionally, performance of an existing contractual duty (but not a duty imposed by law) is sufficient consideration to support a promise from a third party - **Shadwell v Shadwell**. Thus if, for example, a party is contractually obliged to X to unload a ship, doing that unloading is sufficient consideration to support a promise of money from another person.

2   Solution

(a)   In order to be an enforceable contract the terms of the agreement must be certain of meaning.

In **Scammel v Ouston** an agreement for the sale of a van 'on hire purchase terms' was held unenforceable for this reason. Prima facie, then, this agreement between Sidney and Brian is unenforceable as the words 'on the usual terms' are uncertain in meaning.

However, in **Hillas v Arcos** an agreement for the sale of timber which failed to specify the price was held valid because the court was able to refer to previous dealings between the parties in order to ascertain the price. Thus if Sidney and Brian have had previous dealings it may be possible to deduce their 'usual' terms. If this is the situation there is a valid contract between Sidney and Brian.

Furthermore, in **Nicolene v Simmonds** where an agreement was made to sell stated goods at a stated price and ended with the words 'I assume the usual conditions of acceptance apply' it was held that this final uncertain inessential phrase would be disregarded. Thus if the agreement between Sidney and Brian is complete in its essentials without recourse to the phrase 'on the usual terms', the phrase will be severed and a binding contract held to exist of the balance of the agreement.

(b)   In order for a binding contract to exist there must be both offer and acceptance.

An acceptance is the unconditional assent to all the terms of the offer. A counter-offer is an offer made in response to an offer which, being itself an offer may be accepted or rejected by the original offeror. Whichever is the case the counter-offer has the effect of terminating the original offer which is therefore no longer available for acceptance - **Hyde v Wrench.**

Accordingly Brian's counter-offer of £400 terminates Sidney's original offer of £500 and therefore Brian's final statement that he will pay £500 cannot be an acceptance. It is a mere offer. There is thus no binding contract between Sidney and Brian.

(c)   Every simple contract must be supported by consideration and consideration must move from the promisee - **Tweddle v Atkinson.**

Since it is Tom and not Brian who has given consideration there is no enforceable contract between Brian and Sydney.

Furthermore a contract creates rights and obligations only between the parties to it; this is the doctrine of privity of contract - **Dunlop v Selfridge**. If therefore the person with whom Sidney made his agreement was Tom and not Brian lack of privity between Sidney and Brian is another reason for concluding that there is no binding contract between Sidney and Brian

(d)   In order for a binding contract to exist there must be both offer and acceptance.

An offer may be revoked at any time before acceptance and this is so even though the offeror has undertaken to keep the offer open for a stated time - **Routledge v Grant**. However, revocation is not effective until and unless it is communicated to the offeree - **Byrne v Leon Van Tienhoven**. It is not necessary that the offeror himself communicate the revocation: it is sufficient that the offeree knows the offer has been revoked. In **Dickinson v Dodds**, for example, revocation was effective where it was communicated by a reliable third party.

Accordingly Sidney may revoke his offer to Brian before expiry of the allotted 10 days. Sale of the goods elsewhere amounts to revocation. However, that revocation is effective only if Brian knew of it before he stated his acceptance.

Therefore if Brian before acceptance knew of the sale elsewhere there is no binding contract between Sidney and Brian. If, on the other hand, he did not so know there is a binding contract between Sidney and Brian.

3   Solution

(a)   No.

(b)   Georgina has made a counter-offer as she has attached conditions to her acceptance of the original offer and by implication rejected it. It is open to Nigel to accept or reject her counter-offer, and he is entitled to sell the car elsewhere.

4   Solution

(a)   No.

(b)   As a general rule, acceptance of an offer must be communicated by the offeree to an offeror, even where the offeror indicates that he is prepared to waive this requirement. Jonathan has not communicated an acceptance to James, and there is thus no contact between them.

5   Solution

(a)   No.

(b)   Lucy has provided no consideration for Michael's promise to give her the equipment. Consideration is an essential requirement of virtually all contracts, and Michael's promise is not binding.

6   Solution

Mark has the right to claim breach of the implied term as to title under the terms of SOGA 1979. Mark will have to return the car to Henry, but he can recover the full purchase price from Tim.

10   GRANTING CREDIT

1   Solution

Uses a similar benchmark against which all companies are judged.
Facilitates regular review of the credit-worthiness of customers.
Highlights potential areas of concern.
Develops the relationship between the tasks of monitoring credit and establishing credit-worthiness.

2   Solution

Internal information

(a)   analysis of accounts;
(b)   customers in regular contact with current or potential customers.

External sources:

(a)   banks;
(b)   credit agencies.

3   Solution

No. But this information is covered by the Consumer Credit Act 1974.

4   Solution

Debtor collection period $\quad = \quad \dfrac{52,000}{2,500 \times 365} \times 365$ days

$\qquad\qquad = \qquad$ 20.8 days

11   MONITORING AND CONTROL

1   Solution

On demand.

2   Solution

Task 1

A policy that defines, amongst other things, the terms and conditions under which the company grants, controls and monitors credit, decides settlement terms and how it liaises with customers in the credit process.

Task 2

The memorandum should refer to:

- the procedures for granting credit, including such matters as:

    how customers are evaluated for credit (using bank and trade references, historical financial information, press reports, trade journals, credit agency references).

- who may grant credit, authority limits

- the determination of settlement terms

- procedures for monitoring credit

- the relationship between the credit control and marketing functions

Task 3

BARNABY SOFT DRINKS LIMITED

AGED ANALYSIS OF DEBTORS

Customer name	Sales ledger	Credit limit	TOTAL	1-30 days	31-60 days	61-90 days	90+	Other

The 'Other' column may include such answers as "Debit Notes" and 'Unreconciled Cash'. Other acceptable column headings would include 'Current' and 'Risk Category'.

Task 4

Customers may be unable to reconcile the information provided within the invoice to their own records, or be dissatisfied with the delivery of goods or the level of service they are receiving.

Task 5

Good answers will mention:

- a policy of developing a relationship with the customer's administrative staff
- understanding customers' administration procedures
- monitor customer queries
- develop a courteous and firm approach when dealing with all customers

3   Solution

Any THREE from:

- well known and respected locally
- financially sound
- operates a trust account with its bank that is regularly audited and will pay the client promptly
- it is licensed under the Consumer Credit Act 1974.

PRACTICE ASSESSMENT ACTIVITIES

ANSWERS

CASH MANAGEMENT AND CREDIT CONTROL (PREVIOUSLY UNIT 9 AND UNIT 14)

ANSWERS

JUNE 1996

SECTION 1

Task 1

GREENOCK BELTING PLC
1997 BUDGET
DATE OF REPORT ....

Greenock Belting PLC: profit and loss account and cash flow forecast for the year ending 31 July 1997

		£'000
Sales		14,069
Less:	Wages	3,281
	Raw materials and components	5,184
	Production overheads	2,980
	Depreciation	1,400
	Other expenses	300
Operating profit		924
	Interest charged	75
	Other income	325
TOTAL NET PROFIT		1,174
Operating profit		924
	Depreciation	1,400
	(Increase) in trade debtors	(320)
	Increase in trade creditors	64
Increase in production overheads		9
Operating cash flow		2,077
	Interest paid	(200)
	Development expenditure	(125)
	Capital expenditure	(1,500)
	Dividends	100
Net cash flow		352
Opening cash position		(1,773)
Net cash flow		352
Closing cash position		(1,421)

Workings:
Trade creditors: $(5,184 - 4,800) \times 0.1667 = 64$
Trade debtors: $(14,069 - 12,790) \times 0.25 = 320$
Production overheads: $(2,980 - 2,865) \times 0.08 = 9$

Task 2

Potential sources of uncertainty:
- Can sales be made at the (high) forecast increased level of 10% over the next year?
- How stable are the collection patterns, what level of bad debts are anticipated?
- Is there any seasonality in the cash flow?
- Interest rates may change.
- Any tax or dividend payments to be made
- Forecasts of price increases for raw materials and components and wages.

SECTION 2
Task 1

MEMORANDUM

◈ **FOULKS**lynch

To: Chief Accountant
From: Credit Controller
Date: 21 June 1996
Subject: Uses of Credit Insurance

Credit insurance enables organisations to gain insurance against the potential cost of bad debts. This can take the form of insurance for domestic business and export business. The insurance company assumes the bad debt risk in exchange for the bad debt premium.

However, it is not possible for us to unload all our doubtful trade debtors to an insurance company; they will spend a considerable period of time examining our records and systems before they accept any of the risks. Such an examination will consider the overall sales portfolio if cover is provided against the entire sales ledger (a 'whole turnover' policy). It will also consider our credit control system, debt collection procedures and sales ledger administration to ensure we have a robust credit control policy.

Commonly, three types of policy are available:

Whole turnover
These can operate in two ways: (i) to cover our entire sales ledger, although in general cover will usually only extend to 80% of the total insured loss; (ii) to select a proportion of our debtors and insure these for the entire amount. Typically, the insurer will specify a limit beyond which they do not wish to be exposed to unnecessary risk, so we might find there is a limit beyond which we still bear the entire risk.

Annual aggregate excess of loss
With these policies the insurer pays 100% of debts beyond an agreed limit (say £1,000).

Specific account policies
Here, insurance covers a specific debtor for some specific event, such as the debtor being declared insolvent.
Typical premiums for such a policy are usually 1% of the insured sales, with payment normally calculated in arrears and paid in advance in the form of a deposit.

Task 2

(a)   Such historic reports are likely to be out of date, therefore the customer's credit status could have changed dramatically since the date of the accounts; financial ratios calculated even on recent accounts show credit problems often too late for an analyst to act on; aggregation within the group could mean important credit information is lost.

(b)   *Liquidation.* The company is wound up, its assets sold off and closed down.

Receivership. Secured creditors (i.e. those holding a charge on the assets of the business) call the receiver to run the business so they can be paid.

Administration. The court prevents creditors from taking further action against the company, whilst an insolvency practitioner attempts to secure a good resolution

Voluntary arrangement with creditors. The company agrees with the creditors (with the assistance of a practitioner) a way forward to resolve its problems.

Administrative receivership. Rather than liquidating the company the secured creditor could (if they hold a fixed charge) appoint a receiver or an administrative receiver (if they hold a floating charge).

(c)   •   'Warrant of execution' whereby a court orders an enforcement officer or bailiff to seize and sell by public auction goods belonging to the debtor.

•   A 'charging order' which a creditor can obtain on a debtor's property, for example, their house. If the debtor later sells the property they are assured of receiving some of the proceeds.

•   An 'attachment of earnings' which will oblige a debtor's employer to deduct a sum of money from the debtor's wages or salary.

•   A 'garnishee order' enabling money owed to the debtor by a third party (the garnishee) frequently a bank or building society, to be held for the benefit of the creditor.

•   An 'administrative order' whereby a debtor with multiple debts not exceeding £5,000 (at least one of which is a judgement debt that they are unable to settle immediately) to be able to discharge all obligations by making regular payment into court. These are distributed amongst creditors on a pro-rata basis.

•   Petition for bankruptcy in a designated court or the High Court.

SECTION 3

Task 1

Certificate of Deposit

This is a term deposit placed with a bank, in exchange the bank issues a certificate entitling its holder to the money held on deposit plus an interest payment at the end of the stated period. CDs are a marketable security, i.e. the CD holder can sell the CD to another buyer for cash, with the new holder entitled to the cash on deposit and interest, or can sell it on to another buyer.

Task 2

An individual who is the subject of personal data.

Task 3

Money held in a bank account for immediate use.

Task 4

a)   The book debt of the company.

b)   •   Maintenance of the sales ledger
      •   Collection of accounts receivable
      •   Bad debt provision
      •   Finance.

Task 5

Scenario 1

Type of bank borrowing most suitable:

Overdraft facility.

Reason why this bank borrowing is most suitable:

Very commonly used in the retail business. Patch will have a large working capital requirement in the run up to Christmas and New Year. The Christmas and New Year sales should ensure Patch has liquidated its stock and will have sufficient cash to repay its overdraft.

Scenario 2

Type of bank borrowing most suitable:

Long-term loan.

Reason why this bank borrowing is most suitable:

Assets are usually financed with funding of similar maturity. Therefore a ten year asset would be funded with some form of long-term loan.

Task 6

(i)   To the customer - the bank has a duty not to give an adverse opinion without justification. The bank has a confidential relationship with the customer.

(ii)   To the enquirer - a bank can be considered negligent (and liable for damages) if the information it gives is misleading *(Hedley Byrne and Co Limited vs. Heller & Partners Limited 1964).*

Task 7

$$\frac{2}{100-2} \times \frac{365}{60-14} = 16.2\%$$

CASH MANAGEMENT
AND
CREDIT CONTROL
(PREVIOUSLY UNIT 9 AND UNIT 14)

ANSWERS

DECEMBER 1996

SECTION 1

Task 1.1

	January	February	March	April	May	June
Inflows						
Receipts from cash sales	32,800	41,000	49,200	53,300	57,400	68,800
Receipts from debtors	114,800	131,200	131,200	164,000	196,800	213,200
Interest received	925	1,059	646	822	1,064	829
Total inflows	148,525	173,259	181,046	218,122	255,264	282,829
Outflows						
Payments to creditors for purchases	40,000	48,000	48,000	56,000	60,000	60,000
Variable costs	80,000	96,000	96,000	112,000	120,000	120,000
Fixed costs	1,800	1,800	1,800	1,800	2,200	2,200
Advertising		20,000			20,000	
Capital expenditure		90,000				
Corporation tax						56,000
Dividend					100,000	
Interest on overdraft						
Interest on long-term loan						17,500
Total outflows	121,800	255,800	145,800	169,800	302,200	255,700
Net cash flow	26,725	– 82,541	35,246	48,322	– 46,936	27,129
Opening cash balance	185,000	211,725	129,184	164,430	212,752	165,816
Closing cash balance	211,725	129,184	164,430	212,752	165,816	192,945

Task 1.2

(a)   **Receipts and payments method**

- Easy to prepare and understand
- Accurate for short time periods (up to say, 3 months)

(b)   **Balance Sheet or Funds Flow Method**

- Directly related to the organisation's accounting statements and therefore easily reconciled.
- More accurate than Receipts and Payments style forecasts for time periods greater than 3 months.
- Prevent 'nonsenses' such as negative stock etc. occurring in forecast

(c)   **Use of two forecasts together**

The Cash Management section and the Financial Controllers section should be on an ongoing basis, be reconciling differences that arise between the two forecasts to produce a more accurate forecast.

SECTION 2

Task 2.1

(a)   Pay shareholders an increased dividend or make an extraordinary dividend payment.   Consider share repurchase (capital reduction).

Reason:

If no further investment opportunities are to be considered, surplus cash should be returned to shareholders to enable them to seek alternative investment opportunities.   However the firm would be advised to maintain a small cash surplus.

(b)   Invest cash in bank deposits or marketable securities (e.g. CD's, commercial paper).

Reason:

To leave Wilson Ltd with sufficient liquidity to help it make the acquisition, whilst receiving a market return on its cash investments.

(c)   Use cash to make the necessary capital investment in the new product lines.

Reason:

Unless the cash is likely to be needed for a specific reason (such as an acquisition when cash will be needed immediately) it is unlikely that Wilson Ltd will receive a return on its cash investments equivalent to the cost of raising debt finance.

(d)   Hold the cash to make the acquisition; either borrow or raise additional equity finance.

Reason:

The cash will be required for the eventual acquisition at short notice.   The new product lines should be easily financed using external funds.

Task 2.2

Safety	To ensure the securities invested in are of acceptable credit standing.
Liquidity	To ensure the securities have sufficient marketability to allow the maximum availability of funds.
Return	To ensure the securities invested offer a good yield without unduly increasing risk or credit quality.

SECTION 3

Task 3.1

MEMORANDUM

To: **Sales Manager**

From: **Credit Controller**

Date:

Megacorp PLC

Megacorp enjoys a high credit limit from our company, being a key customer to whom we make a high proportion of our sales. However, Megacorp is a poor payer and abuses the 60 days net terms of sale. Ways in which the account might be managed in the future include:

- The use of discounts for early payment or cash sale.
- Develop a better relationship with the customer to ensure prompt payment.
- Consider ways of providing a better service to Megacorp to facilitate prompt payment.

Goodfellows Cycles Ltd

Goodfellows enjoys a relatively high level of credit from our company, of which it does not make excessive use. It is a prompt payer, with the exception of £5,000 which has been outstanding for over 90 days. Ways in which the account might be managed in the future include:

- Settlement of the £5,000 due over 90 days. This possibly relates to a single item, on which there may be a customer query outstanding.
- Find ways of selling more goods to this customer.
- Develop better ways of managing customer queries.

Hooper-bikes Ltd

Hooper-bikes enjoys a medium sized credit limit from our company, which it has abused in recent months. Also it has exceeded its credit limit and urgent action needs to be taken to bring this account to order. Future action should include:

- Ensuring Hooper-bikes reduces outstandings below the available credit limit.
- Considering reducing the credit limit.
- Considering ways of improving Hooper-bikes' payment record.
- Considering reducing sales to Hooper-bikes.

Dynamo Cycles Ltd

Dynamo Cycles enjoys only a modest credit limit from our company and has a good payment record. In the future we could consider:

- Increasing sales to Dynamo.
- Increasing Dynamo Cycles' credit limit.

Task 3.2

WILSON LTD TRADE REFERENCE FORM

STRICTLY CONFIDENTIAL

To: *Name of Trade Referee*
            Address of Trade Referee

Name of Potential Customer

1.	How long have you traded with this firm?	.... months*
		.... years*
		Many years*
2.	How much credit do you usually allow?	£
3.	What are your payment terms?	Pro-forma*
		Monthly*
		.... days*
4.	Are payments generally made to your satisfaction?	To terms*
		Up to 1 month late*
		More than one month late*
		Very slow irregular*

5.   Any other information will be appreciated

....

....

....

....

....

....

....

Signed: .... Date ....
*please delete where inapplicable.

CASH MANAGEMENT
AND CREDIT CONTROL
(PREVIOUSLY UNIT 9 AND UNIT 14)

ANSWERS

JUNE 1997

SECTION 1

Task 1.1

End of year	Start of project (0)	1	2	3	4	Total
Sales						
Production (trays)		15,000	25,000	35,000	45,000	120,000
Sales (£)		78,750	137,813	202,584	273,489	692,636
Payroll costs						
Project leader		21,200	22,472	23,820	25,250	92,742
Driver		11,660	12,360	13,101	13,887	51,008
Trainee costs		135,680	143,821	152,450	161,597	593,548
Payroll		168,540	178,652	189,372	200,734	737,298
Other operating costs						
Maintenance		1,838	2,481	3,184	3,951	11,454
Utility costs		3,120	3,245	3,375	3,510	13,250
Land rent		1,924	2,001	2,081	2,164	8,170
Fertiliser		1,575	2,756	4,052	5,470	13,853
Minibus costs		2,625	2,756	2,894	3,039	11,314
		11,082	13,239	15,586	18,134	58,041
Equipment costs						
Portakabin	7,000					7,000
Protective clothing	800	840	882	926	972	4,420
Rotavators	3,300		1,819			5,119
Minibus	10,000					10,000
Other tools	1,000					1,000
Irrigation	5,000					5,000
	27,100	840	2,701	926	972	32,539
Opening cash flow	0	(27,100)	(128,812)	(185,591)	(188,891)	
Total cash flow	(27,100)	(101,712)	(56,779)	(3,300)	53,649	
Closing cash flow	(27,100)	(128,812)	(185,591)	(188,891)	(135,242)	

Task 1.2

Options include EITHER forms of external funding:

- government grants (including job creation grants, development funding etc.)
- charitable donations
- bank loans

OR internal finance (from EKAT) using inter-company loans etc. to fund the project.

In practice, funding may come from a variety of sources. It is important to recognise the need for financial prudence and the need to reduce financial (and business) risk given EKAT's stated objectives and the nature of the project. Government/charitable funding is most appropriate, with external bank loans, leasing, factoring etc. most likely to be inappropriate given the not-for-profit motive of the organisation.

SECTION 2
Task 2.1

EKAT Aged Debtor Analysis – 31st May 1987 – Credit terms: 30 days

Action
1 Statement
2 1st reminder
3 2nd reminder
4 Telephone call
5 Warning letter
Recovery action implemented

Customer name and ref	Total amount	Invoices not yet due	Outstanding 1 month	Outstanding 2 months	Outstanding 3 months	Outstanding 3+ months	1	2	3	4	5	6
Gartcosh	£10,000	K521 £5,000		K496 £5,000			03-Apr K496	03-May K496				
Strathaven	£6,600	K511 £6,600										
Coatbridge	£5,775	K505 £4,000			K411 £,000		03-Mar K441	03-Apr K441	03-May K411			
New Mains	£14,000	K508 £2,775		K487 £2,000		£8,000 K289	03-Jan K289 / 03-	03-Feb K289	03-Mar K289	03-Apr K289	03-May K289	
Castlemilk	£11,000			K472 £11,000			03-Apr K472	03-May K472				
Rutherglen	£1,000			K481 £1,000			03-	03-May K481				
Cambuslang	£1,500					£1,500 K204	03-	03-Jan K204	03-Feb K204	03-Mar K204	03-Apr K204	03-May K204
Easterhouse	£16,000	K510 £3,000		K392 £13,000			03-Apr K392	03-May K392				
Airdrie	£2,750					£2,750 K234	03-	03-Mar K234	03-Apr K234	03-May K234		
Stewartfield	£5,000	K513 £5,000										
TOTALS	**£73,625**	**£26,375**		**£32,000**	**£3,000**	**£12,250**						

Task 2.2

Gartcosh

A good customer that appears to take over 60 days to make payment. Consider ways of encouraging prompt payment, e.g. settlement discounts.

Coatbridge

A large customer seemingly abusing their credit terms at the expense of a small supplier (EKAT). Consider ways of improving relationship and obtaining prompt payment, e.g. provision of settlement discount.

New Mains

A particular problem seems to exist with invoice K289 and invoice K287 is outstanding for 2 months. Establish whether a query exists with the invoice regarding quality or service. If there are no problems, consider ways of enforcing payment, using the legal process or a debt collection agency.

Cambuslang

A small customer with one outstanding invoice (K204). Establish whether this is in dispute. If not enforce payment using the legal process or a debt collection agency. Be prepared to write-off the debt.

Airdrie

Establish why K234 has been part-paid. Investigate why action has not been taken to recover this earlier. Negotiate with Airdrie for full payment.

SECTION 3

$$\frac{2.5}{97.5} \times \frac{365}{(60-7)} = 17.66\%$$

Task 3.2

Two of the following:

- to reduce the cost of the administrative effort in collecting it

- to reduce the risk of default

- to reduce the cost of funding if it is likely that such a customer will make late payment

- to improve its cash flow

Or other reasonable answers.

Task 3.3

EKAT

EKAT,
29, Glen Arroch,
East Mains,
East Kilbride,
G74 7C0

Ms Margaret Darroch,
Director of Finance,
Canadian Steel Corporation (UK) Ltd.,
Summerhill Street,
Coatbridge,
Lanarkshire,
ML12 6TY.

20 June 1997

Dear Ms Darroch,

INVOICE NO: J548
Total amount outstanding. £1,634.93

Despite previous reminders and telephone calls, we have still not received your payment in settlement of the above invoice. You have promised payment on a number of occasions but no payment has been received to date.

We regret that, due to the above, we have no alternative but to consider the Small Claims Procedure in the County Court in order to recover the sum outstanding. Prior to us taking such action we would however wish to give you one final opportunity to make payment. We will therefore delay submission of the claim to the County Court for a period of <u>seven days</u> from the date of this letter, in the hope that the account is settled. We will not enter into further correspondence regarding this matter other than through the County Court.

Please note that, if we are forced to take legal action, you may become liable for the costs of such action, which, if successful, may affect your future credit rating.

Yours sincerely,

A Competent-Technician

Task 3.4

- Customer account no.
- Customer account name
- Customer address
- Action taken (e.g. telephone, fax, letter, who spoken to, date and time)
- Date payment promised
- Amount promised
- Details

Task 3.5

Any five from:
- acts as banker to UK central government
- responsible for the issuance of bank notes in the UK
- deals with government borrowing
- intervenes in foreign exchange markets
- banker to the commercial banks
- is a lender of 'last resort' to the banking system
- acts as an advisor to the government on monetary economic policy
- acts as agent for the government in carrying out its monetary policies
- sets interest rates

Task 3.6

An overdraft is repayable on demand. With a bullet repayment loan the principal is repaid in one payment at the end of the loan.

CASH MANAGEMENT
AND CREDIT CONTROL
(PREVIOUSLY UNIT 9 AND UNIT 14)

ANSWERS

DECEMBER 1997

	£000 Jan	£000 Feb	£000 Mar	£000 April	£000 May	£000 June	£000 Total
Opening position	(27,000)	(27,158)	1,684	(22,308)	(42,438)	(37,686)	
Tourism	10,000	14,000	14,000	14,000	20,000	20,000	92,000
Shipping	(20,000)	(10,000)	(17,000)	(15,000)	(15,000)	(12,000)	(79,000)
Ship trading		25,000					25,000
Capital Expenditure			(15,000)				(15,000)
Taxation			(6,000)				(6,000)
Dividends				(11,000)			11,000
Interest on loans				(8,000)			(8,000)
Interest on overdraft	(158)	(158)		(130)	(248)	(220)	(914)
Interest on cash surplus			8				8
Closing position	(27,158)	1,684	(22,308)	(42,438)	(37,686)	(29,906)	

Task 1.2

Any five from:

- cancel dividend
- raise additional equity
- negotiate further debt
- sell assets
- cancel capital expenditure
- bring forward cost cutting plan
- reduce stocks (inventory)

Task 1.3

Any two from:

- exceeding the overdraft limit

- receipt of £25 million from sale of ship (e.g., from delays in negotiations, lack of finance for the purchaser, collapse in ship values etc).

- the uncertainty of receipts from tourism.

Task 1.4

- easy to take, that is, the lender clearly has security over the asset by holding the title to the secured property.

- easy to value; the secured asset should have a clearly identifiable value

- easy to realise; the asset can be readily convertible into cash.

SECTION 2

Task 2.1

MEMO

To: **Credit Controller**

From: **Accounting Technician**

Date: **5 December 1997**

Subject   **Castle Ltd's request for credit**

Bank references are a useful source of information: but banks are naturally cautious. The prospective customer (Castle Ltd) is the bank's client, to whom it owes a duty of care. The bank also owes a duty of care to the inquirer (ourselves) and can be considered negligent if the information it gives is misleading. A negligent statement is made without reasonable grounds or is ambiguous.

Therefore, banks are naturally cautious about the terms they use. The bank reference provided by National Bank plc is not encouraging as the bank has made no reference to the credit asked for (i.e. £25,000 on 60 days terms). The indication that resources are fully employed is not encouraging. A more favourable reference would indicate they were 'considered good for your figures' or were 'undoubted'.

The trade references are less clear. The first is from Windsor Haulage Ltd which has been trading with Castle Ltd for just over a year. When they opened their account with Castle Ltd, no suitable trade or credit references were supplied, indicating that they were newly established or that Windsor Haulage Ltd have very unsophisticated credit granting procedures. The terms of their credit to Castle Ltd are different to those requested (monthly as opposed to the 60 days net of the present request).

The reference from Case Western Shipping Inc is more curious. The company appears to have been trading with Castle Ltd for over three years. However, unlike Windsor Haulage Ltd, they did receive trade and credit references. The amount of credit granted is also significantly higher (£65,000 as opposed to the £25,000 requested from us). Case Western Shipping Inc also indicate that Castle Ltd is their largest customer. This may influence the content of the reference, i.e. they may feel obliged to, even though the reference is confidential, as well as the fact that given they are prepared to offer such credit terms they are unlikely to admit to offering credit to a bad payer.

The contradictions within the trade references and the modest bank reference indicate that we should investigate further. Other sources of information should be used and followed up. We should also liaise with our sales and marketing team, who can indicate how important a potential customer Castle Ltd is. If credit is granted, caution should be urged, perhaps by reducing the credit terms granted to 30 days net and, if practicable, indicating a lower monetary limit.

Task 2.2

None. Data subjects must be individuals, not corporate bodies and information must be held on computer.

Task 2.3

- the success of attempts to collect the debt

- the expense of pursuing the debt

- the likelihood of insolvency proceedings and communication from liquidators or administrators as to the probability of payment.

Task 2.4

A factoring agency administers a client's debts by:
- keeping the books of account for sales, ie a book-keeping service for the sales ledger
- sending out invoices to customers
- collecting outstanding monies from debtors
- credit control

SECTION 3

Task 3.1

			£ million
Extra profit:			
(a)	Increase in sales revenue	(120 million x 10%)	12
(b)	Increase in profit	(£12 million x 15%)	1.8
	Total sales revenue	(£120 million + £12 million)	132
Extra investment:			
Average debtors		($^3/_{12}$ x £132 million)	33
Current average debtors		($^2/_{12}$ x £120 million)	20

Increase in debtors	13
Increase in stocks	1
	14
Decrease in creditors	1

(c)	NET INCREASE IN WORKING CAPITAL	15

(d)   *Return on extra investment:* 1.8 million ÷ 15 million   12%

(e)   Return on extra investment is less than 20%, therefore NOT worthwhile.

Task 3.2

- trade practice or custom
- to improve sales and profitability
- allow customer the opportunity to inspect goods or services purchased for correct quality.

Task 3.3

Seasonal differences are short term fluctuations in recorded values, due to different circumstances that occur at different times periods, e.g. of the day, of the week, or year, e.g Shops might expect higher sales in November and December, because of Christmas.

Cyclical changes are medium term changes in results caused by circumstances which repeat in cycles, e.g. in business, cyclical variations are associated with economic cycles, excessive booms and slumps in the economy.

Task 3.4

(a)   An index is a measure over time of the average changes in the values (prices or quantities) of a group of items. An example is the Retail Price Index, which measures changes in the cost of items in an average household.

(b)   Index numbers are useful in forecasting cash flows as, if production volumes are assumed, then costs can be calculated with projections based on an appropriate index.

CLASS ACTIVITIES

QUESTIONS

1–2   CASHFLOW AND CASH BUDGETS

1   Activity

Data

You have recently been appointed to a position in the cash management section of the accounting department at Stenwater Limited, a marine construction contracting company based in Aberdeen.   The company was formed by the merger of two local companies eighteen months ago and it has been experiencing some administrative difficulties following the rapid expansion of business.

From your work so far, you are aware that Stenwater's procedures for managing the cash collection process are rather basic and some improvements could be made.

Task 1

Some time has now passed and Stenwater's cash management procedures have become more sophisticated. You now personally prepare weekly and monthly cash flow forecasts in 'receipts and payments' style format.

As these forecasts are short-run with most items occurring in the near future, many managers believe that financial transactions over this period could be forecast very accurately.   What FOUR categories of transactions might create the sources of uncertainty which make short-term cash flow difficult to forecast? Give an example of each.

Task 2

Stenwater's cash flow is typically very seasonal with the maximum borrowing requirement in the summer months. From the graph below it can be seen that the maximum borrowing is expected to occur in June.

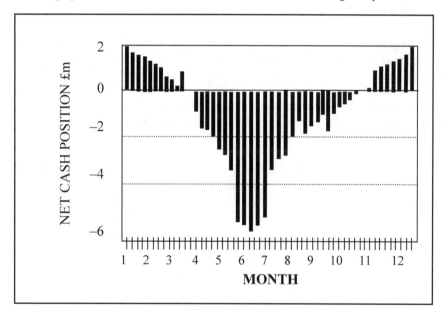

STENWATER FORECAST CASH POSITION

It is crucial that the peak borrowing requirement is identified and monitored.

The Finance Manager has suggested monitoring cash flow by a series of moving averages. Calculate the 3-day moving average for the series of cash flows given below.

Date	Net Cash Position (£ million)	3-Day Moving Average (£ million)
6 June	(5.351)	–
7 June	(5.415)	–
8 June	(5.451)	
9 June	(5.587)	
10 June	(5.654)	
13 June	(5.487)	
14 June	(5.478)	

Task 3

(a)   When does the net cash position trend cross the 3-day moving average?

(b)   What does this indicate?

Data

Kirkton Jeans Ltd started in business on 1 November 200X with share capital of £200,000. It received £100,000 in enterprise grants from a Regional Enterprise Company and has negotiated a £325,000 overdraft facility from a local bank.

The company is a fashion manufacturer specialising in the manufacture of denim jeans for the domestic market. At the commencement of business the company bought cutting and sewing machinery costing £130,000 and fixtures and fittings of £11,000

Kirkton Jeans will sell a small range of denim jeans, each with a similar cost structure and sold at a similar price:

	£	£
Selling price		15.00
Costs:		
Direct labour	6.50	
Direct material	3.25	
Variable overheads	1.50	
		11.25
Contribution		3.75

Fixed overheads are property expenses of £240,000 per annum, paid monthly in advance, and energy costs of £115,200 per annum, paid quarterly in arrears in February, May, August and November. Other fixed costs are estimated at £15,000 per month, to be paid monthly.

Forecast sales are as follows:

Nov	Dec	Jan	Feb	Mar	Apr	May
Nil	20,000	24,000	24,000	22,000	20,000	26,000

The planned production profile is as follows:

Nov	Dec	Jan	Feb	Mar	Apr	May
24,000	24,000	22,000	20,000	26,000	26,000	28,000

50% of sales are for cash. The remainder are credit sales. Industry experience and market research suggests that all credit sales will be paid in the month following sale, ie, "net monthly."

Material purchases are paid for in the month incurred.

Variable overheads and direct labour are paid for in the month they are incurred.

The bank charges interest on overdrafts at the rate of 1% per month, calculated on the closing balance at the end of the month. Interest is then paid on the first banking day of the following month.

Tasks

(1)   Using the proforma cash flow budget which follows, prepare a month-by-month budgeted cash flow forecast.

(2)   What are the advantages and disadvantages of using cash flow forecasts in receipts and payments style as prepared in Task 1?

Task 1

KIRKTON JEANS LIMITED

	Nov	Dec	Jan	Feb	Mar	Apr	May
RECEIPTS							
Cash sales							
Credit collections							
Share capital							
Enterprise grants							
Cash income							
PAYMENTS							
Direct labour							
Material purchases							
Variable overheads							
Property costs							
Energy costs							
Other fixed costs							
Capital costs							
Interest							
Cash outflows							
Net cash flow							
Balance b/f							
Balance c/f							
Sales							
Production							

3   Activity

Cash flows can be classified between regular revenue receipts and payments and infrequent or irregular receipts and disbursements.

Give an example of each of the following:

(a)   A regular revenue receipt

(b)   An exceptional payment

(c)   A capital payment

(d)   An annual disbursement

3   FORECASTING TECHNIQUES

1   Activity

Annual sales of Brand Y over the last eleven years have been as follows:

Unit sales of Brand Y, Year 1 – Year 11 (thousands)

Yr 1	Yr 2	Yr 3	Yr 4	Yr 5	Yr 6	Yr 7	Yr 8	Yr 9	Yr 10	Yr 11
50	59	46	54	65	51	60	70	56	66	76

Task

(a)   Calculate a **three-year** moving average trend.

(b)   Plot the series and the trend on the same graph.

(c)   Produce a sales forecast for Year 12, stating any assumptions.

Task

(a)   Convert the GDP series to index numbers with Year 6 = 100.

(b)   Calculate deflated index numbers for GDP and average gross earnings, with Year 6 = 100.

(c)   Plot the two deflated indicators against time on the same graph and to comment critically upon the meaning of these data.

2   Activity

The data below refer to Average Earnings Index numbers in Great Britain for different sectors of industry, 2002 = 100, and the Retail Price Index, 2001 = 100.

Date	Whole economy	Production industries	Service industries	Retail price index
2002	100.0	100.0	100.0	107.0
February 2003	104.6	104.9	104.4	111.5
May 2003	107.5	108.1	107.2	115.0
August 2003	109.1	109.2	108.7	115.8
November 2003	112.8	112.9	112.7	118.5
February 2004	114.0	114.3	113.7	120.2
May 2004	118.5	118.2	118.6	126.2
August 2004	120.9	119.7	121.1	128.1
November 2004	123.8	123.7	123.0	130.0

Date	Whole economy	Production industries	Service industries	Retail price index
February 2005	124.7	125.2	123.8	130.9
May 2005	128.1	129.2	127.1	133.5
August 2005	130.8	130.2	130.4	134.1
November 2005	130.8	131.8	129.7	135.6

(Source: Employment Gazette)

Task

Using 2002 = 100 as base throughout, deflate the Production Industries Index and comment briefly on the real (inflation-adjusted) change in its average earnings over the period 2003-2005.

4–5   THE ECONOMY AND BANKS

1	Activity

Briefly explain the difference between:

(a)   a standing order and a direct debit;

(b)   a credit card and a debit card.

2	Activity

The Bank of England was founded in 1694 and has evolved to perform a number of functions. Describe TWO of these functions briefly.

6–8   TREASURY AND RAISING FINANCE

◇ FOULKS*lynch*

1   Activity

Negotiable instruments are documents used in business to secure payment of money. Give TWO examples of commonly used negotiable instruments.

2   Activity

Differentiate between 'With Recourse Factoring' and 'Without Recourse Factoring'.

9   BASIC LAW OF CONTRACT

1   Activity

Anna bought a pair of shoes from Wonder Shoe Shops Ltd. Three weeks later, the heel of one of them fell off, although Anna had only worn them three times, in normal conditions.

Is Wonder Shoe Shops Ltd in breach of any of the implied terms of the Sale of Goods Act 1979, and, if so, which?

2   Activity

Average overdue debt for UK companies reached a record £145,000 in the first quarter of 1994.

(Source: *Trade Indemnity plc)*

£20 billion is overdue to private businesses at any one time with an average payment period of 2.5 days.

(Source: *Forum of Private Business)*

Although remedies exist for breach of contract created by late payment of debt why are businesses reluctant to use the force of law? Identify TWO issues.

10   GRANTING CREDIT

1   Activity

Data

Salon Select Limited supplies hairdressing consumables to the hairdressing business in Scotland and North East England from its base in Glasgow. Salon Select has been approached by Crocodile Cuts, which operates a chain of hairdressers, to supply goods for its five shops. Crocodile Cuts has asked for credit of £20,000 on 60 days terms and has supplied a bank reference and two trade references. You have written to the bank and the trade referees and their responses are set out on the next three pages.

Strathclyde Bank plc

Argyle Street Branch,
501 Argyle Street,
Glasgow,
G2 7LT

```
Credit Controller
Salon Select Limited,
1, Weaver Street,
Glasgow,
G2 90P

19th May, 200X

Dear Sir or Madam,
```

Reference–Crocodile Cuts Limited

I refer to your letter dated 10th May 200X enquiring about the credit worthiness of the above. In our view Crocodile Cuts is reasonably constituted and should prove good for your figures.

```
Yours faithfully,
```

G. Donarski

```
Gerald Donarski,
```
Manager.

SALON SELECT LIMITED,
1, Weaver Street,
Glasgow,
G1 9OP
(0141-203-3197)

PRIVATE AND CONFIDENTIAL

Credit Controller,
Black Fred-The Barber's Friend Limited,
27, Westminster Terrace,
Glasgow
G3 4EF

10th May, 200X

Dear Sir or Madam,

We recently received a request from Crocodile Cuts Limited, a customer of ours, who gave yourselves as a reference. I would be grateful if you could assist us by answering the following questions and returning them in the stamped addressed envelope provided.

1.   How long have Crocodile Cuts been trading with you?

    __**2**__years   _____months

2.   When Crocodile Cuts opened an account with you did the company supply you with suitable trade and credit references?

    YES   /   (NO)

3.   What are your normal credit terms for Crocodile cuts:

    Amount: __**£10,000**__

    Terms: Cash | Monthly | Weekly   Other (please detail below)

    ....

    ....

4.   Does Crocodile Cuts make payments in accordance with your terms?

    (YES)   /   NO   /   SLOW PAYER

5.   Have you ever had to suspend credit facilities to Crocodile Cuts?

    YES   /   (NO)

    If YES when?

6.   Please supply any other information which you consider relevant.

Thank you for your help,

Yours faithfully

B. Diamond

Bruce Diamond,
Credit Controller

SALON SELECT LIMITED,
1, Weaver Street, Glasgow, G1 9OP
(0141-203-3197)

PRIVATE AND CONFIDENTIAL

Credit Controller,
John Mathieson,
19, St. Mary's Court, Hyndland,
Glasgow,
G11 7UN

10th May, 200X

Dear Sir or Madam,

We recently received a request from Crocodile Cuts Limited, a customer of ours, who gave yourselves as a reference. I would be grateful if you could assist us by answering the following questions and returning them in the stamped addressed envelope provided.

1.   How long have Crocodile Cuts been trading with you?

       __3__ years   _____ months

2.   When Crocodile Cuts opened an account with you did the company supply you with suitable trade and credit references?

       YES   /   (NO)

3.   What are your normal credit terms for Crocodile cuts:

       Amount: _N A._

       Terms: Cash   [Monthly]   Weekly   Other (please detail below)

       . . . .

       . . . .

4.   Does Crocodile Cuts make payments in accordance with your terms?

       YES   /   NO   /   SLOW PAYER   _N/A_

5.   Have you ever had to suspend credit facilities to Crocodile Cuts?

       YES   /   NO   _N/A_

       If YES when?

6.   Please supply any other information which you consider relevant.
                   We have been supplied by Crocodile Cuts now for 3 years
                        and we are very happy with them.
Thank you for your help,

Yours faithfully

B. Diamond

Bruce Diamond,
Credit Controller

Task 1

Study the references on the three pages before this and consider Crocodile Cuts' request. Recommend how salon Select should proceed.

Task 2

What other information could Salon Select seek on Crocodile Cuts and how would it use this information? Identify TWO other items and how they would be used.

Task 3

Credit rating agencies provide information about businesses to enable their creditworthiness to be evaluated by a supplier. The information supplied by such agencies could be categorised as Legal Data, Commercial Data and Credit Data.

Describe TWO items of information you might expect to find in each of these categories in a typical agency report.

(i)   Legal data

(ii)   Commercial data

(iii)   Credit data

Task 4

As most of the information provided by Credit Reference Agencies is publicly available, why do you think companies use them?

---

2   Activity

From the following data, calculate the Days Sales Outstanding.

31 March	Total debtors	£4,987,500
March	Sales	£2,493,750
February	Sales	£2,244,375
January	Sales	£2,493,750

11   MONITORING AND CONTROL

1   Activity

The diagram below illustrates the credit cycle in terms of cash flow:

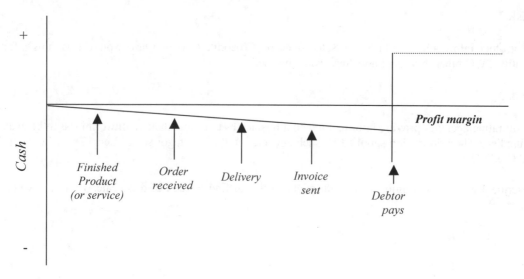

The credit control function usually concentrates on reducing the time between payment and invoicing.

How may a company achieve improved credit control before the invoice is despatched?

2   Activity

Collection activity can be improved by taking a more proactive approach to credit control. Regular contact with a customer's administration staff can identify problems in the customer's systems.

(Source: 'Effective Credit Management' *Accounting Technician*—October 1994)

Identify THREE typical (legitimate) problems for the customer that can create delays in collection.